THE SKILLS OF DICTATION

THE SKILLS OF DICTATION

Eva Roman

Gower

First published 1971 by Gower Press Limited as *The Art of Dictation*

This edition published 1990 by
Gower Publishing Company Limited
Gower House
Croft Road
Aldershot
Hants GU11 3HR
England

Gower Publishing Company
Old Post Road
Brookfield
Vermont 05036
USA

ISBN 0 566 02908 1 2nd edition
(ISBN 0 7161 00851 1st edition)

Printed in Great Britain by
Billing & Sons Ltd, Worcester

Contents

Acknowledgements   viii

Preface   ix

PART I: DICTATION PROCEDURE

1   **Characteristics of good dictation**   3

2   **Organization of material and examples**   8
    Example of logical preparation for a dictation sequence

3   **Examples of dictation routines and practice**   12
    An example of dictation routine – A large industrial
    concern: notes for dictaters – A commercial concern: notes
    for guidance on the use of the remote control equipment –
    An insurance and underwriting concern: notes for dictaters –
    A local government department: memorandum from medical
    officer of health to all members of the health department

4   **Instructions to the typist**   23
    Instructions for letters – Instructions for memos – Draft
    reports – Tabulations

5   **Posture and delivery**   25

6   **Timing**   28

7   **Corrections**   31

v

PART II: INSTRUCTIONS ON STYLE AND PUNCTUATION

8   Text organization   35
Writing a letter – Tabulation – Headings and indents

9   Spelling problems and the phonetic alphabet   40
Method – Capital letters

10 Punctuation principles   43
The full stop – The comma – The semi-colon – The colon –
Parentheses – The hyphen – The question mark –
Quotation marks – Capital letters – The exclamation mark –
Brackets, inverted commas and underlining

11 Money and figures   53

12 List of words which sound similar   55

PART III: SPECIMEN DICTATING PROCEDURES

13 Business letters   59
Example 1 – Example 2 – Example 3

14 The internal memo   66

15 The draft report   71

16 The finished report with special layout instructions   74

17 Tabular material   78

18 Dictation on to preprinted forms   81

19 Instructions for word processing applications   84
Edited draft – Programmed correspondence

PART IV: INSTALLATION OF A DICTATING SYSTEM

20 Note form dictation   89

21 The input stage to word processing   91
Checklist of some word processing applications

22   The importance of dictation equipment   94
Types of equipment – Checklist for action

23   The text processing manager   97
Rules for dictaters – Rules for audio secretaries

Index   100

Acknowledgements

I wish to express my appreciation for valued collaboration received in the preparation of this book from Mr Glyn Richards JP and Mr Roger Fuller, Sales and Marketing Manager, Sony (UK) Ltd. A special thanks to Peter King in appreciation of his humour and skill in creating the cartoons.

Eva Roman

Preface

Much water has flowed under the bridge since the introduction of the book *The Art of Dictation* in 1971. Dictation machines and centralized systems have become more sophisticated, and manufacturers are concentrating on the input side of text processing with much refinement in equipment design and functions. Machines have become more computerized.

Research has shown that, today, few organizations produce correspondence without the use of some form of dictation medium. It is widely appreciated that conventional shorthand dictation can waste up to 40 per cent of time for both dictater and transcriber.

There are advances too at the other end of dictation – the production of correspondence – by use of integrated systems such as word processing equipment, photocopiers, fax, electronic mail, and so on.

However – whatever equipment is used from the note taker to the very latest computerized centralized system – methods of dictating have changed little. Authors still need to pay attention in order to produce trouble-free dictation and instructions to the transcribing secretary.

Many different job titles are now given to staff at the production end. Those working in a text processing centre, typing pool or any small puddle may be referred to as audio typists, text processing operators, word processing operators or correspondence secretaries. Those who work for one manager may well be called secretaries, personal assistants, audio secretaries, and so on. In the interests of simplification, the term 'audio typist' is used preferentially throughout this book and may represent any of these variants. Also, although it is recognized that increasing numbers of males are entering secretarial professions, for convenience the terms 'she' and 'her' are used to denote either sex. Equally, managers are referred to in the male gender; this in no way is meant to presuppose that all managers are male and is retained for the purposes of simplification. The use of these stylistic 'abbreviations' is not intended either as a comment on, or a reflection of, the relative status of men and women in the business world.

It won't bite!

One item of initial advice: do remember, if you know who is to transcribe your work, to use her name at the beginning, and during, dictation. This really does make the audio relationship much more personal and friendly. After all, you will be communicating with her person-to-person, through the medium of the machine.

PART I

DICTATION PROCEDURE

1 Characteristics of good dictation

The success of any dictation installation, whether by means of individual machines or the more complex centralized system, depends to a very large degree on cooperation between the dictater and the audio typist. If, after coordinated training, the two departments – the executives and the typists – achieve a real partnership, the organization's correspondence and efficiency will do it credit.

Such a partnership is not easy to attain. It is necessary that certain essential rules should be appreciated and observed. A failure to abide by them can lead to confusion of the audio typist which can, in its train, bring unfortunate and time-wasting results. Thus, before venturing into the main content of the letter, instructions to the typists should be clear, concise and convincing.

Obviously the first rule, where a multi-user dictating system has been installed, should be for the dictater to identify himself and his department and telephone extension number. Failure to take this elementary precaution, especially in a large organization, can create delay because any recorded medium, whether tape, disc or belt which arrives in a text processing centre without being capable of quick identification is in a limbo – it will not find its way back to the originator for signature and dispatch. It is not enough to expect the typist to identify the voice of the dictater, nor fair to expect it.

There are, of course, cases where dictaters announce their names and, having given this brief introduction, plunge into their message, feeling that their basic duty has been done. This can prove over-hasty, especially if there are errors in the dictation and the typist needs to contact the dictater by telephone to elucidate the point. She may have to telephone several people and departments to locate him.

In cases of special layouts the dictater should make a point of informing the audio typist what he wants and how he wishes it to be carried out.

3

It is helpful, too if she is instructed at the outset what length the correspondence is likely to be – short, medium or long. If no such indication is given the dictater may well find short letters typed on A4 paper or, conversely, a fairly long letter which could have been contained on an A4 sheet running on to a number of small sheets. This applies especially in the case of business organizations which use several sizes of letter heading, and it is wasteful.

It is essential, too, before she starts, for the typist to be told how many copies the dictater requires. This is best specified at the start, as 'original and … copies'. If this vital information is left out the typist may assume that it will be the usual 'one plus one' and she will have good reason to be annoyed if, at the end of a long spell of dictation, she reaches the surprising announcement, 'Oh, by the way, I require … copies'. Either the whole piece has to be retyped, which is time-consuming and prevents other people's dictation being typed promptly, or costly photocopying must be resorted to.

In every typing centre the supervisor will make provision for really urgent correspondence to be typed first if there is an audio typist available, or to give it to the first available girl. It is therefore most important to give a verbal indication at the very beginning that the work is wanted without delay. If the indication of urgency is stated at the end of the recording sequence it is virtually meaningless because the typist is unaware of it until the transcription has been done, probably in its due turn in accordance with the rotation of normal correspondence. Care should, of course, be exercised to establish that only really urgent letters should be so described and thus obtain priority. A true respect for the rule that only urgent work should be nominated as such ensures a fair deal for all.

When advancing into the body of a letter/memo/report, further instructions need to be given from time to time. This point is dealt with in later chapters, but in general the dictater must keep in mind, when giving his instructions, that it is very easy for an audio typist to mistake the instruction for actual dictation – with sad results. It is therefore most helpful to the typist if the dictater pauses slightly before giving an instruction and also alters the tone of his voice. To make quite sure that what follows is instruction and not dictation, precede it with the explanation, 'Typist please …'. Any audio typist who puts this on to her transcription should hide her head in shame!

If a confidential piece of dictation needs to be typed the supervisor should be informed. She may well type it herself or give it to a senior typist who is accustomed to undertake the confidential work.

Should it be necessary to send files to the typing centre the fact must be made quite clear by means of a special instruction so that the typist can 'marry up' the recording medium with the file. This also applies to any enclosures which might need to go with the correspondence.

The essential points to remember before commencing dictation are:

No need to shout

1   Identify yourself by name, department and telephone extension number.
2   Make sure that you give instructions about the number of copies.
3   Inform the audio typist of any special layout.
4   Mention the length of your dictation.
5   Say whether there are any files to be 'married up' with the recording.
6   Say whether the correspondence carries enclosures.
7   Indicate verbally at the start whether the correspondence is urgent.
8   Precede any instruction with the words, 'Typist please ...' or, if the name of the transcriber is known, use it.

The dictation system is a machine but the audio typist is human. Machine and typist can produce the best results only when due regard is paid to the fact that the scope for error is considerable if the intentions of the dictater are shrouded in a fog of assumptions. The audio typist should never be expected to be a mind reader. By all means credit her with intelligence, but don't put an undue strain on it. The machine imposes a discipline on her but she cannot respond to it unless the dictater is also disciplined in his approach to what he wants done.

Speech into the telephone or microphone should be by way of the ordinary speaking voice – neither shrill nor low. Many people have the idea that the audio typist cannot understand any dictation unless it is loudly expressed and/or spoken very slowly. Both practices are undesirable. Speaking loudly can produce distortion and unduly slow speech can be an irritant to the typist who has developed a certain speed and rhythm of transcription.

Equally at fault is the dictater who tries to maintain a speed of 180 words a minute. He is not running a race and the audio typist, even the fastest and most experienced, cannot equal such a speed.

If speech is too fast, the words tend to suffer through slurring. The little words such as 'if' and 'but' are often swallowed up and this has the effect of producing incoherence. In most instances it tends to alter the intended sense of the correspondence.

Avoid monotony

Unduly rapid speech can also make nonsense of a communication. The all-important word 'not' which is sometimes the dominant word in a sentence can be missed by the audio typist, with disastrous results if the omission is not observed in the finished product.

The pitch of the voice is all-important as is the speed of delivery. The undue lowering of the voice cannot always be compensated for by the audio typist turning up the volume of her machine, even to its maximum. Nor should the dictater raise his voice unnaturally. The louder the speech the greater the amount of distortion, and no amount of volume control on the machine will eliminate it entirely. A natural speaking voice with its normal cadences without extremes of pitch will always come over more effectively.

The dictater should also bear in mind that dictation in a monotonous tone heard through a pair of earphones for, perhaps, a long period can be very boring indeed. At worst it can induce a half sleep in the audio typist. The workflow produced from a reasonably animated voice will be livelier and help to keep the typist's interest at all times. Therefore, when dictating correspondence, remember:

1   to speak in a natural voice
2   to speak neither too slow nor too fast;
3   not to shout or whisper;
4   to speak with feeling and emphasis.

2 Organization of material and examples

The dictater should try to act as though the audio typist were present in the room though, of course, she is not. The instrument into which dictation is given cannot ask questions, give reminders or offer helpful suggestions. Thus, the instructions that are essential to produce a satisfying piece of transcription must be explicit and full. (For details of this, see Chapter 4.)

First, the dictater must have a tidy and clear desk; clear, that is, of all the items which are not involved in his intended spell of dictation. He should then gather the material needed in connection with the dictation – the necessary files, data, memoranda, correspondence, plans, graphs and so on to which reference may have to be made. Having sorted them as far as maybe into the order in which they may be needed, he can proceed with confidence, assured that he can refer to necessary information at the right time and place.

An additional aid to fluency is to make short notes or headings regarding the matter about to be dictated. A well organized line of thought is a time-saver, as well as providing a better finished product. When the rough notes have been made they should be checked over to see if the subject matter is being dealt with in the correct and logical way. If it is seen that one part of a letter or report will need greater precision of expression the inclusion in the notes of the appropriate words will prove a great help during the actual dictation. Remember:

- the machine cannot ask questions, so be precise;
- speak as if person to person or face to face;
- do not clutter your desk with unnecessary papers during dictation;
- have all correspondence and files within easy reach;
- make headings to aid an easy flow of dictation.

Having decided to embark on a spell of dictation it is advisable to organize this in a natural sequence:

Short notes?

1 Always try to deal with your correspondence in small batches.
2 Deal with three to four items on one recording at one time.
3 Plan what you want to say before commencing the dictation:
   (a) assemble the facts;
   (b) be clear about the contents which you wish to dictate;
   (c) select the right approach;
   (d) prepare a plan.
4 Choose the simple word, use simple brief sentences and have one idea to a paragraph.
5 Do not get the 'I's and the 'we's mixed.
6 Make sure that the close ties up with the opening.
7 Remember: Dear Sir, Yours faithfully, or Dear Mr/Mrs, Yours sincerely.
8 Always call the supervisor if you require help with your dictation or need assistance in using the system.

Example of logical preparation for a dictation sequence

Systems in various offices differ with respect to the method and timing of dictation. Most sizable firms and large local authorities using an audio typing system have their own house rules which, though they may not differ greatly in essentials, are tailored to their own requirements. However, the following sequence provides a practical starting-point.

1   Obtain file of previous correspondence

2   Make sure all relevant information about the requested products is to hand

3   List products in order of sequence

4   Make heading notes on paragraphs

5   Before commencing, check reference

Ref ABAK/UV/10479
A B Jones & Co Ltd
456 Old Briar Mead
London W12

6   Heading as recipient's

Dear Sirs,
Re PBE 44 Copper Bins

7   Refer to correct date of recipient's letter

Thank you for your inquiry dated 12 May on further quantities of copper bins from our new range.

8   Give audio typist instructions on layout

Section 1

PBE 44

The new range of copper bins is at present in short supply but we hope to be able to send substantial quantities to our wholesalers in about six to eight weeks. The above mentioned product will be priced at:

(a)   Half-inch thick coating £12 per doz

(b)   Quarter-inch thick £10 per doz

9 Check previous correspondence for former requests to
prevent repetition

As mentioned in our previous
correspondence, the PBE
range will be further
extended in the next few
months and we shall keep
you informed about any new
items.
Yours faithfully,

3 Examples of dictation routines and practices

Different organizations have varying rules regarding the sequence in which dictation should be done and, for this reason, it is not possible to be categorical about the order in which a dictater should work.

Some companies have their letter headings designed in such a way that it is a simple exercise to follow each stage of dictation. Whether to dictate the details of the addressee before commencing the text of the letter or to place them at the end of the letter depends on the practice of the organization concerned. Some organizations use 'window' envelopes which require that the name and address of the addressee should be located on the page so that, when folded, it appears in the 'window'.

The following hints on dictation sequence and routine can, therefore, be suggestions only, to be adapted as required to conform with the house rules of an individual organization.

An example of dictation routine

Start the recording by informing the audio typist of:

1 Your name, department and telephone extension number.
2 The correspondence requires an original and ... copies.
3 The dictation is a letter/memo/report/....
4 Short/medium/long items of dictation.
5 Any files to be linked with the recording.
6 Any special layout or spacing instructions, etc.

12

An example of sequence of dictation

Letters	*Memos*
Your reference	To
Their reference	From
Addressee	Copies to
Dear Sir/Dear Mr, etc.	Reference
Heading	Subject
Text	Text
Salutation	Name of signatory
Name of signatory and	
department	Enclosures
Enclosures	
Copies to	

Before replacing the instrument, end with the words, 'End of dictation, thank you'.

Below are variants on the plans supplied to dictaters and supervisors by three large business concerns and a local government department. They are offered only as a guide but they show that, in order to secure the best results, it is desirable that some plan should be distributed to those who are concerned with personal dictating systems.

1 A large industrial concern: notes for dictaters

General

Dictation will be recorded through a separately wired telephone receiver, to centrally positioned dictating recorders.

Hours of operation

The system will operate for typing during normal working hours. Outside these hours – lunchtime and evening – the dictation system will still be available. The supervisor may not be in attendance to answer queries, but the 'fast bleep' will be audible indicating that you are connected to a dictating recorder. All typing after 1500 hours will be given the date of the following day, unless requests are made to the contrary.

Start early

Dictation procedure

Dictate as early in the day as you can. Typists could be waiting for work in the morning and be under pressure later, often causing delays in the return of work.

To facilitate availability of dictating recorders for other users the receiver must be replaced after dictating six letters. This will ensure a faster turnover of work by spreading the load over all typists.

Should you wish to carry on with dictation lift receiver again to select another machine.

When familiar with dictation practices do not replay dictation unnecessarily. This wastes time and reduces availability of dictation recorders for other users.

Paragraphs 1, 2 and 3 emphasize the need to be aware that dictating recorders are being shared by all users and any time-saving techniques will help maintain the overall efficiency of the system.

Before starting dictation collect all relevant papers and make notes where necessary to assist continuity of dictation.

When dictating, to help the typist:

1   Identify yourself.
2   State whether report, draft, memo or letter, giving number of copies required (excluding original and file copy). Indicate type and size of paper where possible, such as A4 (210 x 297mm) or A5 (148 x 210mm).
3   Give punctuation – commas, full stops and new paragraphs.
4   Pronounce unusual names or words and spell out, for example: Lea–Leigh, Stephen–Stevens, and all foreign names.
5   Give figures and amounts of money very clearly.
6   Give brackets or inverted commas both before and after.
7   Instruct typist on layout of tabulations.
8   Preface any instructions during dictation with 'Typist ...'.

External letters

1   State your name and department.
2   Give type and size of paper and number of copies required.
3   State 'our' reference, 'your' reference and your GPO telephone extension number.
4   State 'For the attention of ...' if required.
5   Form of address – Dear Sir/Madam or Mr.
6   Subject heading if required.
7   Text of letter.
8   End letter with 'Yours sincerely' or 'Yours faithfully' and your name and title when used.
9   Name of firm and full address including county and postal code.
10 Copies to ....

Internal memos

11 State your name and department.
12 Give type and size of memo paper and number of copies required.
13 Give 'from' name and reference.
14 Give 'to' name and reference, and postal code.
15 Subject heading if required.
16 Text of memo.
17 Copies to ....

Reports

18 State your name and department.
19 Give type and size of paper and number of copies.
20 State whether draft (double spacing) or finished report.
21 Text of report.

22   Copies to ... .

2 A commercial concern:
notes for guidance on the use of the remote control equipment

The equipment is available from 08 30 to 17 00 hours.

Instructions to dictaters

1   Announce yourself by name, internal telephone number and department.
2   Indicate whether your dictation is a letter, memo or report/draft.
3   Indicate whether you are sending any files to the typing centre or if there are to be any enclosures (for right size of envelope).
4   Give any special instructions, for example, spacing, layout, personal or confidential. *Note*: When dictating confidential work please dial 0 on completion of your dictation and advise the supervisor.
5   Indicate all capitals, punctuation, paragraphs; commas should be indicated by the tone of voice, but stops, paragraphs and less obvious punctuation should be given.
6   Preface all instructions during the course of dictation with the words, 'Typist please ...'.
7   Spell out unusual names and words – that is, names of towns, people, technical words, commonly misspelt words such as those which could be spelt in more than one way.
8   Make sure that the close suits the salutation.
9   *Very urgent work.* When you have finished your dictation, and before replacing your handset, dial 0 and advise the operator. She will then ensure that your tape receives priority. Please confine this service to really urgent letters.
10   In the event of very lengthy spells of dictation (reports) individual machines will be used in place of the centralized system.

Dictation plan

1   Keep dictation to small batches – four or five items at a time as a maximum. 'Little and often' should be the rule.
2   Decide what you want to say before lifting the receiver.
3   If the subject is difficult or complicated, jot down major points and paragraph headings to guide you.
4   Be brief.

Sequence of dictation

Letters	*Memoranda*
Number of copies	To/from
My reference	Number of copies
Your reference	Heading
Addressee	Text
Dear Sir/Mr or Mrs	Designation of signatory
Heading (if required)	Copies to
Text	
Salutation	
Designation of signatory	
Copies to	

Always call the supervisor if you need help during dictation or if you are not sure how to use the service in any way.

3 An insurance and underwriting concern: notes for dictaters

Careless dictation will cause delay and difficulty to both experienced and inexperienced typists, resulting in incorrect and badly typed transcription and dissatisfaction to the dictaters and typists. Clear and careful dictation makes for speed and efficiency and good relations all round.

Here the opportunity is taken to mention that no matter how new or inexperienced the dictater is to the insurance business, its terms and jargon, in a short time he or she will manage to assimilate a certain amount of knowledge of underwriting. A typist has little or no knowledge of under-writing and though she may have knowledge of insurance terms, she can still only type what she hears. Pressure of work does not allow her time to substitute one word for another or look up spellings of proper names or addresses which have not been given.

It will be agreed that quickness and clarity of thought both in dictation and transcription is a gift not everyone is endowed with; therefore, it is suggested that until users of the system are confident of their ability to dictate clearly, and without losing track of the meaning of a letter, a rough draft should first be made as a guide.

1   *Dictate as early as you can.* This ensures an even flow of work. If this is not done, typists are often waiting for work early in the day and under pressure later on, with the result that letters are typed care-lessly and errors made which go unnoticed.

It is also beneficial to the writer to dictate in the early morning. If he leaves it till mid-morning, when all the machines are being used, he then has to wait until one is available.

The machines will be switched on to 'Automatic' for dictation after normal hours, but since there will be no contact with the typists, the dictater's department, reference and telephone extension must be dictated.

2   *Department, reference and telephone extension* will already have been given when contact has been made with the typist. This should be followed by stating size and type of paper, whether air mail, number of copies required and size of envelope, if a large one is needed. The typist does not know the size required for every enclosure to a letter. The size of paper is not always known, but in the *majority of cases there is some idea.*

3   If a letter is to be despatched by air, it should be stated whether it has an enclosure. The typist will then use the correct type of paper.

4   'Messrs' should be used when the firm is not a limited company.

5   Spelling of proper names and addresses is essential; use the phonetic alphabet to distinguish between difficult letters such as B and P or T and E.

6   State reference of letter under reply.

7   *Mode of address.* This is typed before the heading. Therefore, if it is other than 'Dear Sir/s' or 'Madam', for example 'Dear Mr Smith', *inform the typist before dictating the heading* or she will have already typed 'Dear Sir'.

8   *Headings* should be dictated in a uniform manner, claim numbers being included and *not* typed under the dictater's reference.

9   The name of the month should be used and not 'instant', 'ultimo', etc.

10   *Punctuation.* Dictate paragraphs and full stops. Other minor punctuation is a matter for the dictater to indicate if he so wishes.

11   *Quotations, breakdown of premiums and the like.* If these are included in the body of a letter it must be made clear to the typist if the calculations are to be set out in the form of a sum.

12   When four items have been dictated, redial for another typist.

13   Letters to be corrected in the typing department should be altered in *pencil* on the *carbon copy* and *not* on the top copy.

14   *Urgent* letters should be dictated as early as possible and the supervisor advised. She will then arrange for them to be given priority.

15   The dictater should state if any particular letter is required the same day, as all letters typed after 16 00 or 16 15 will be dated for the following day.

16   *Statements and schedules.* Thorough instructions should be given to the typist – size of paper, headings of columns, and so on. Alternatively, the dictater should come to see the typist to explain what he requires or bring in a previous layout if there is one. Time spent on the latter alternative will be repaid by the speed of dictation and appearance and accuracy of the finished work.

17   If a dictater is interrupted and has to stop for any length of time, he should either finish the letter he has started or contact the typist telling her he will finish his dictation later. This will keep the machine from being idle and make it available for use by someone else.

18   No one appreciates loyalty to the typist more than the supervisor, but it is hardly loyal to allow typing of a low standard to go out to the public or to a titled official of the company for signature, bearing in mind the typist's initials are on the document or letter. Therefore, any complaints or suggestions should be made to the supervisor who will investigate these fairly.

4 A local government department: memorandum from medical officer of health to all members of the health department

Introduction of audio typing

1   Audio typing will be introduced into the department as from .... The cooperation of all members of the staff is requested from the outset to ensure the efficiency of the system.

2   Detailed 'operating instructions' are attached. The company providing the new equipment will give instructions and advice to all staff prior to the installation and for the first few days of operation.

Dictating instructions

3   (a)   The aim must be to retain the use of the equipment for the minimum essential period and not keep it 'occupied' when not in use for actual dictation. To this end, relevant papers should be collected in logical order, and notes made to assist fluent dictation.

(b)   Please give all dictation in a clear normal voice directly into the mouthpiece. Make sure the ends of words are clear, particularly those ending with s, and try to make consonants clear. For example, emphasize the difference between f and s, b and v, b and p, d and t, m and n and w and r. You must also be careful with the pronunciation of figures to make sure that thirteen is not mistaken for thirty, fourteen for forty, etc. Do not run words into one another.

(c)   Specify any punctuation, particularly paragraphs and full stops. Indentations should also be specified whenever applicable and in this connection see paragraph 5.

(d)   Spell unusual names, addresses and words, and use the phonetic alphabet to clarify letters.

(e)   At the commencement of dictation give your name, your section and your telephone extension, and state whether there are any supporting papers (see paragraph 7 hereto).

(f)   Give any special instructions required, for example, whether the communication is in the form of a draft, an internal memorandum or an external letter, and state if any extra copies are required, and, if so, the distribution.

Dictation sequence

4(a)   For internal memoranda:
1   From (name or title of sender)
    To (name and title of addressee)
3   Your reference
4   Their reference
5   Subject heading
6   Text of memorandum

(b)   For external letters:
1   Telephone extension number
2   Your reference
3   Their reference
4   To (name and address of addressee)
5   Form of address, for instance Dear Sir/Madam/Mr – or Sir
6   Subject heading
7   Text of letter
8   Salutation and title of signatory

5   It is intended during the next month or so to compile a manual containing specimens of various work of the department, which will assist dictater and typist, especially in the setting out of dictation. This manual, it is hoped, will contain a specimen of all routine documents produced by the department, and any suggestions as to what should be included therein should be submitted to the chief administrative assistant.

6   When an extra copy of a letter or memorandum is required to send to someone other than the addressee, you should dictate appropriate instructions. The typist will then mark the yellow copy 'Copy sent to Mr ... for information' and will produce a further copy marked 'Copy – to Mr ... for information'.

Supporting papers

7   Where it is necessary to send supporting papers to the typist, for example for copy typing of lengthy extracts from documents, these should be placed in a special re-usable folder, supplies of which can be obtained from the typing supervisor. These folders must be sent to the typing centre with an appropriate slip attached (which will be supplied) which will enable the typist to relate the papers in the

folder to the dictation tape. The typist will not (in normal circumstances) commence typing until the supporting papers have been received, and on completion of the work the folder will be returned with the completed work to the dictater, via the dispatch section (see also paragraph 8).

8   The audio typist will not collect papers or documents from offices, or return them on completion of typing. The dispatch section will collect work from the typing centre at the following times during the day: 1000, 1200, 1445, 1530 and 1600. All typing work in the typing centre will be allocated by the supervisor and any queries regarding the operation of the equipment or the typing work must be directed to her.

9   It must be remembered that the typist will work completely 'blind'. The dictater will get back from the typist exactly what is put on to the tape! The onus is on the dictater to explain precisely what is required. In the past, a shorthand typist could ask questions of the dictater at the time of dictation, but, quite obviously, this will not be possible under the new system.

10   (a)   The installation must be used intelligently, and priorities if any,

Supporting documents

will be restricted to a minimum. The ideal is to dictate as and when you can – even if it is only a two-lined memo. This will make for a quicker turnround of work. The system or the individual machines *must not be 'monopolized'*, so that they can be put to the best possible use at all times. Records will be maintained of the time a machine is engaged and released and of the actual dictation time so that cases of abnormal usage can be investigated.

(b) A record will also be maintained of the use of the individual desk machines. Users of these machines must make a note on the index slip of the time the machine is used for that particular dictation, so that this information can be included in the records to be maintained by the typing supervisor.

11 Copy work will continue as at present, but full instructions must be written on all work sent to the typing centre, that is number of copies, paper size, stencil or plate, and including the originator's name and telephone number.

12 The success of the system will depend to a great extent upon the cooperation of all members of the staff in complying with these instructions, and I am sure all concerned will do their best to assist in this respect.

4 Instructions to the typist

Most dictaters are in the habit of dictating to shorthand typists and in turning to the machine tend to act as though it were a secretary. This is a mistake. The machine gives a faithful record of what is spoken into it – errors included – whereas a shorthand typist can question at the time of dictation and any necessary alteration or amendment can be made there and then. The machine is as versatile as the dictater who uses it.

The audio typist has a right to expect that the dictater has practised the operation of the equipment so thoroughly that he can use it properly and fully benefit from its efficiency. If he has absorbed the principles of good dictation his task, and more especially that of the audio typist, is so much easier.

It is helpful to the dictater as well as to the eventual recipient of the dictation if the normal courtesies are observed. A cheerful 'Good morning' or 'Good afternoon' is a useful and happy introduction; it is rather demoralizing for an audio typist to hear a disembodied voice coming through her earphones and barking 'Brown here – letter to …'. The polite approach takes the formality out of the mechanical operation.

When giving instructions to the audio typist, the use of words like 'please' and 'thank you' make all the difference to the attitude of the girl towards the dictater on whose work she is currently engaged. The establishment of a rapport between them is mutually advantageous and improves the quality of the work.

The following examples show the various types of instructions which might be used during a dictation session covering letter layouts, memos, draft reports or tabulations.

Instructions for letters

(a) 'Good morning, typist. I require a letter please with … copies; no special layout but the envelope to be large enough to include two sets of literature. Thank you. Letter begins …'.

This is the most straightforward type of letter to be dictated and, apart from the normal spelling and punctuation instructions, needs no further directions except those on distribution of copies.

(b) 'Good afternoon typist. This letter with ... copies is to contain several paragraphs of different product descriptions. Would you please give a sub-heading for each separate product and further indent each following paragraph by four spaces. There will be six different products. I also require the heading to be typed in full capitals.

There will be a folder of correspondence for reference. Letter begins ...'.

Instructions for memos

'Good morning typist. This is Mr ... here, department ... telephone extension number. ... Would you please type a memo to ... with ... copies. These are to go to. ... I am sending Xerox copies of ... to the typing centre in my folder which must be included with each memo to the different staff members. Memo begins ...'.

Draft reports

'Good afternoon. Mr ... speaking, of ... department, telephone number .... The following is a medium-sized draft report. Major paragraphs will start on the left of the paper but all sub-sections will be indented three spaces from the margin. Paragraphs to be numbered, sub-sections to be in roman numerals. Will you please use double spacing. I only require one copy at this stage. Thank you. Report begins ...'.

Tabulations

'Good morning typist. In this letter I am going to include a small tabulation consisting of six columns. The size of each column is as follows: column 1, 2½ cm wide; column 2, 2¼ cm wide; column 3, 4¾ cm wide; column 4, 4¾ cm wide; column 5, 1 cm wide; column 6, 8 cm wide.

'Headings for each column are as follows .... This requires ... copies.'

5 Posture and delivery

Surprising as it may seem, a dictater who is seated comfortably is a better and more composed dictater, yet there are some who work in conditions not conducive to logical thinking. Their laden desks, littered with material that has no immediate connection with what they are currently doing, adds to the air of confusion. It is not unknown for the receiver to be wedged between the neck and ear, while the dictater sits on the corner of his desk.

At the outset the telephone or dictating machine must be so sited that no bodily contortions are necessary in using it. It is also common sense that the chair in which the dictater is sitting is at a comfortable height in relation to the desk.

Many dictating machines have an automatic volume control which maintains a fairly constant volume of recording even though the dictater may speak softly or loudly, or even move away from the machine. It is unwise, however, to place too much reliance on this. Speaking at a constant level at a distance of four or five inches from the microphone produces better results.

Some people imagine that the flow of inspiration is improved if they walk about during dictation sessions, others that their output is the better if they have a cigarette or pipe between their lips. These, however, are handicaps to good recording and often mar what might otherwise have been a clear dictation. A good posture and organized methodical arrangement will save the dictater backache, headache and fatigue and therefore enable him to produce a better finished product. Without them the dictation can emerge as something like the following:

Good morning. Please take a letter to Mr [bus passes by] – close that window Miss Hopkins. Dear Sir, Thank you for your letter of the [rustle rustle] January – paragraph – I am sorry that [bang] do you have to make so much noise? Where was I? Oh yes, the [suck suck] matter is receiving – come in Mr Smith, I'm just finishing this dictation, take a pew old man –

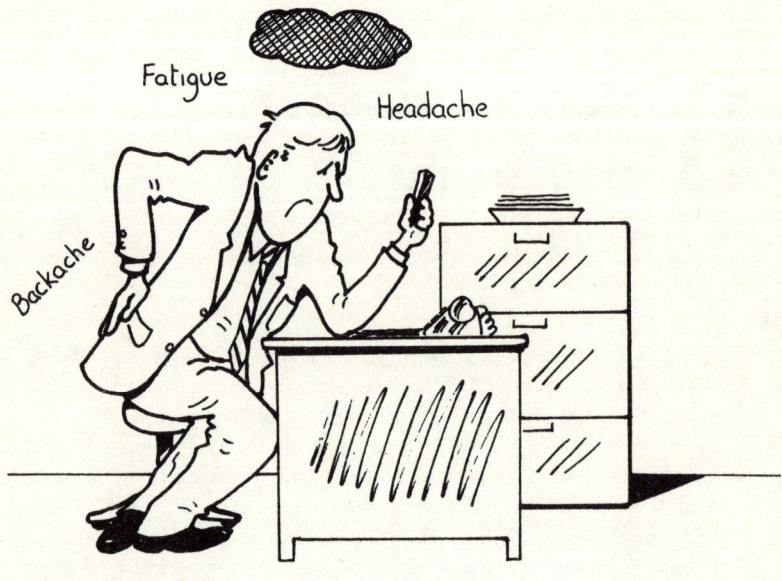

Correct posture

our consideration — yes, two sugars, Miss Hopkins. Your faithfully, etc, etc.

It would be an extremely skilful audio typist who could identify what was relevant from this sample, for it is obvious that the dictater would have directed his speech away from the mouthpiece whenever he digressed to address another person. Thus, the flow of his dictation would have fluctuated very much.

The way a dictator holds his handset or microphone is a matter of some importance. It is designed to suit the shape of the human head and should, therefore, be held to conform to its design. Contortions on the part of the user bring distorted results.

While the receiver is wedged behind the ear or tucked under the chin its distance from the mouth prevents it from singling out the speaker's voice as the dominant sound. It tends to pick up extraneous sounds such as doors banging or even the conversations of other people, not to mention the sounds created by the dictater's other occasional mouthpiece — his pipe. It is not difficult to imagine the effect on the audio typist. In most instances she will be forced to give up guessing and ask the dictater to pocket his pipe during his next spell of dictation. In short, hold the handset or the microphone at the correct angle and at the right distance from the mouth, so that the dictation will be clear to the audio typist. Therefore, in order to maintain correct posture and delivery:

1   Clear the desk of all unwanted material.
2   Place the machine in a position of easy reach and operation.
3   Ensure that the chair is at the correct and comfortable height.
4   Speak at a constant level with the instrument four to five inches away from the mouth.
5   Refrain from putting anything into your mouth while dictating.
6   Direct your speech straight into the mouthpiece or microphone, not to the side of it.

Irritating background noises

6 Timing

The dictater who familiarizes himself with the instrument he is to use will be concerned to know exactly how to start and stop it at will. There are various reasons why he will have to stop the recording – an interruption by a visitor, the demands of the telephone, the need to seek some item of information which was not laid on his desk prior to the commencement of the dictation or any such reason.

As previously noted, the first essential in any spell of good dictation is to make sure that all the relevant papers are at hand so that no searching is needed in the course of the dictation. Even so, it is not always possible to compose a complete piece of dictation without a mental search for the appropriate words or phrases. The more fluent may find that the necessary sentences come to mind quite easily, but others discover that they have to stop to think.

When it becomes necessary to decide what to say next, and how best to say it, the machine should be stopped so that there is no long silence on the recording medium during which the typist has to listen. This interrupts her rhythm, as well as requiring, in most instances, that she has to repeat part of the recording to obtain the sense of continuity from the previous dictation.

The dictater controls the machine and, when he wants to refresh his memory by looking up data, or if an interruption takes his mind off the subject, he should immediately stop the machine and start it again only when he is mentally equipped to continue. If, even then, he has to go back on what he has already recorded in order to listen to his last few phrases he can do so readily and thus add the previously elusive sentence without impairing continuity.

Care should, however, be exercised when stopping and starting to make quite sure that word endings are not clipped by stopping the machine too soon. The same can, of course, happen when dictation is being resumed. Speech should begin only when the machine has fully started its recording cycle.

Many people, when engaged in normal conversation, create pauses at sentence or phrase endings. These pauses become even more pronounced when reading from correspondence or reports.

It is important when talking into a microphone or handset to make natural pauses at the ends of phrases or sentences because by doing so the typist is enabled to retain an even flow during her transcription. Equally important is the fact that by providing himself with these pauses the dictater gives himself a valuable aid in the event of having erred on a question of fact or of grammar if there has been a slip of the tongue.

If a correction (see Chapter 7) should become necessary in the course of dictation it can be carried out in such a way that the typist need never know that a mistake has occurred. If the dictater has left pauses at the end of phrases or sentences he can go back to the end of his last correct sentence and stop the machine at that point. He then resumes dictation with the new corrected sentence over the faulty one, since, by overrecording, the previous speech is automatically erased.

There is, of course, no need to exaggerate the pause by a long silence as this might easily give the typist the false impression that the dictation has

The quick stop

ended. The more natural the speaking and pausing the better the typist's flow of transcription will be.

To make the fullest correct use of the instrument:

1   Familiarize yourself with the stop and start controls.
2   When an interruption occurs, stop the recording medium.
3   Never let the tape run on without recording.
4   Always be in full control of the machine.
5   Make sure that, when stopping the machine, the last word of the recording is not clipped by switching off the machine too soon.
6   When resuming recording, make sure the machine has started its recording cycle before resuming speech.
7   Leave natural pauses at phrase and sentence endings.
8   Remember that natural pauses help the audio typist to obtain an even workflow.

7 Corrections

A common occurrence during any dictation session is that of the small error due to some slip or abstraction. Few people can say that there have not been times when they lacked concentration or were not disturbed in their train of thought, leading to a word, date or minor point being mis-dictated. Whenever such an incident occurs the dictater should make use of the facility to overdictate (as indicated in Chapter 6), but it should be an absolute rule never to attempt to replace a single word in the middle of a sentence with another. Almost invariably, the last half of the preceding word also manages to find its way into the correction or half a word of the correct dictation is lost.

A dictater may be replaying his recording in order to check that all is well. He may indeed find that the text is not to his satisfaction and wishes to alter a sentence. It would, of course, be wasteful to erase much of the recording which is quite satisfactory merely to correct one sentence. Possibly a major insertion is found to be necessary but one cannot, of course, insert additional matter between previous recordings. In such a case it is best to wait until the end of the letter and then to inform the audio typist by means of an instruction mark or its equivalent that a major correction needs to be carried out at the appropriate place. The typist will always listen to the special instruction or the equivalent means of identification prior to typing the content and will thus know beforehand that there are corrections to be incorporated.

If an item of dictation has many corrections it may, in some instances, be a wise course for the dictater to inform the supervisor as perhaps circumstances prevent him from re-dictating. In this way special care will be taken to ensure correct transcription.

Having grown accustomed to using individual machines, or indeed remote control systems, the dictater sometimes tends to grow overconfident in his approach to the system. Little but necessary instructions are left out and the essential habit of preparing a dictation plan is omitted.

It is for the dictater to examine his own technique in the light of the fact that the typist can commit to paper only that which he has put onto her machine in the first place. In such circumstances the dictater must become his own critic. When a piece of dictation has been completed he should play it back (or as much of it as is necessary) to assure himself that all essential facts have been covered, and take a form that will leave the recipient in no doubt as to what he is trying to convey.

This is not to suggest that it should be a common practice that every time a piece of dictation goes to the typing centre it should previously have been monitored by the dictater. Nor is it suggested that the audio typist should have to devote her time to listening to a spell of dictation prior to typing as a guarantee against possible errors.

If a self-critical attitude is adopted from time to time by listening and yet the correspondence is still imperfect, then it is time to engage the aid of the systems supervisor who is responsible for cooperation between all the parties involved. By adopting the 'be your own critic' attitude the dictater can ensure that the use of the system is a success and that understanding and liaison between management and typing centre do not fail.

Rules to observe are:

1   Avail yourself of the facility to overdictate.
2   Never attempt to replace a single word with another in the middle of a sentence.
3   In case of major corrections inform the typist by means of an instruction mark or equivalent.
4   In the event of many corrections within the body of one letter always inform the supervisor of the fact to avoid confusion.
5   Always adopt a self-critical attitude by playing back parts of your recording.
6   Discuss problems with the supervisor.

PART II

INSTRUCTIONS ON STYLE AND PUNCTUATION

8 Text organization

Before beginning to write or dictate, the author should have clearly in mind what he wants to say. It is equally important that he should have an idea of the sequence in which he wants to say it.

If the letter is intended to reply to one received, care should be exercised to quote the heading which it may bear. This helps to ensure the identification of the subject at the receiving end. In this way, the author, being quite clear about the content of the document, will not find it difficult to compose a suitable reply.

Writing a letter

Preparation

Before beginning to write a letter, be sure:

1 you know what you want to say;
2 of the sequence in which you are going to say it;
3 of all the relevant facts when replying to correspondence;
4 that each separate sequence will form a paragraph.

Headings

A heading will be beneficial:
1 if your correspondent has already used one, as you can then use the same heading in your reply;
2 if it helps to shorten the letter;
3 if, by using one, it helps to identify the subject quickly;
4 if you are beginning correspondence leading to a sequence of letters on the subjects.

The form of address

If you know the name of your correspondent use it. If, however, the name is not known, address the correspondence to the company, for the attention of the individual.

The opening paragraph

Always make clear the reason why you are writing the letter in the opening paragraph. If a heading has not been used, it will help to identify the subject.

Use simple terms, avoiding old-fashioned phrases like: 'Your favour of 10th inst to hand re alterations'.

Always make the division of paragraphs clear to the audio secretary by giving her instructions: 'Full stop – new paragraph'.

Body of the letter

This is the important part by which you succeed or fail to create understanding in the mind of the recipient of your letter. The object is to convey information, problems or questions which you may have by using simple language. You may know the dictionary backwards but it would be unfair to assume that the reader is equally well informed. Therefore remember:

1   Be as brief as is consistent with covering all necessary points.
2   Cover the subject of your letter in logical sequence.
3   Each subdivision of the subject should form a separate paragraph.
4   Make your sentences short.
5   The use of punctuation can enhance the understanding of the recipient of your letter. However, by keeping lengths of sentences to approximately 12–18 words, punctuation can be kept to a minimum.
6   In certain cases it may be useful to number points to avoid overlooking important matters.

Final paragraph

Avoid repetition in your closing paragraph. Do not use stereotyped and meaningless endings such as:

'Awaiting the favour of your esteemed command' or
'Assuring you of our best attention at all times'.

Always make sure that the recipient of your letter knows what action to take once he has read your letter. Never leave him in doubt about the next step. Failure to do this can sometimes hold up important information or make it necessary to communicate by telephone.

Always let the audio secretary know when you come to the end of your letter. It can be frustrating and time-consuming listening to empty tape just in case ....

Checklist for 'before and after'

1 Before you write it:
   - Is my letter and the time it involves really necessary? Or would a telephone call be more efficient?
   - Do I have all the relevant information, documents, etc to help me compose the letter?
   - Do I know exactly what I wish this letter to convey?
   - Do I know the logical order?
2 Before you post it:
   - Does the letter contain *all* I want to convey?
   - Have I covered the contents in a logical sequence?
   - Is the letter easy to read?
   - Have I made clear to the reader what action he/she should take?
   - Would I be favourably disposed toward the writer of such a letter?

If you are satisfied that you can answer *yes* to all the above questions, pass the recording to the audio secretary for transcription.

Tabulation

It is true to say that everything can be dictated, but it may not always be the most economic way of presenting the work to the typist. In some organizations it is common practice to compile long and complicated figures in a form which cannot be standardized. This may be due to complex details which are difficult to explain verbally. In such cases a dictater needs to do a certain amount of research which may take several days before all the essential information is at his disposal. At the end of the compilation everything has to be put down on paper and possibly checked and rechecked before it can go to the typing centre.

This type of tabulation will be most uneconomic to dictate into a system. Broadly speaking, anything which needs to be written out first should qualify for copy typing.

At the other end of the scale is the small tabulation in the body of a letter or report which can always be dictated. But before embarking upon this kind of tabulation there are several important points to be observed in order to produce a tabulation with full instructions which will leave the typist in no doubt as to the dictater's intentions.

It should be remembered that the audio typist in the centre can be contacted and the dictater's problems regarding tabulation can be fully discussed during the recording just as would be the case if the girl were actually in the room with the dictater.

The dictater should visualize how a typewriter functions. The typist types from left to right and then proceeds to the next line. Thus, for column dictation matter should always be dictated across the page – never down a column with the expectation that the typist should go back to the top of the second column on the right hand side of the page. This may cause the typist to miss the first line and the whole tabulation goes amiss.

It is important, too, to inform the typist about the width of each column. If she hears an instruction for four columns she will assume that they are of equal width. If there is to be a variation in width she must be informed of the measurements.

When the content of each column is being dictated and there has been an indication given that there are to be four columns, the typist will expect four entries to be dictated – one for each column. Therefore, if there is no entry for a particular column the dictater must instruct the typist accordingly, otherwise a wrong entry may well be made in the empty column.

Whenever possible it is advantageous to make use of the glossary idea. If a standard form is in existence the typist will find it a valuable aid to give her an idea of what the tabulation will look like when finished. Four points need to be remembered:

1   Indicate the number of columns required.
2   Inform the typist about the width of each column.
3   Always dictate the contents of the columns across the page.
4   In the event of a line not having an entry in a column, indicate this by saying 'Typist please – no entry in the next column'.

Headings and indents

At some time during the dictating of correspondence the need arises for the use of some form of heading. It may be in answer to a letter from a customer where the dictater wants to refer to a question already raised or it may well be desirable when writing about some person or, indeed, in correspondence from accounts departments.

Whatever the purpose of the heading the dictater will need to inform the typist. If his dictation concerns a report, memo or routine letter of standard layout no further instruction will be necessary in relation to the heading, as the typist may be considered competent enough to use her own initiative on the application of standard practice.

If, however, the dictater wants to deviate from the standard layout he should say so and instruct the typist on the nature of the heading. He may wish to have this placed either on the right or the left side of the notepaper or indenting may be required. Even the normal central siting of the heading should be indicated.

It is useful for the dictater to think carefully about the information the typist needs to have in order to make an attractive layout of headings. In some cases the headings may be of such a length that they require more than one line of typing. Where does the break come? How has the dictater visualized it? He knows what he wants and it should not be left to the typist to accept the responsibility of expressing his unspoken thoughts. This might cause her to produce the wrong result and even change the sense of the heading.

Therefore, the dictater must always indicate the content of each line individually if a heading involves more than one line of typing. A three-line heading should be dictated in this form:

'A three-line centre heading please
First line ...
Next line ...
Last line ...'.

The use of this method guarantees that there will be no room for doubt as to where every single word belongs.

9 Spelling problems and the phonetic alphabet

It is becoming fairly general practice in most typing centres to devise a glossary of unusual words in common use in that concern (but not necessarily in universal use) names and addresses and any other information which will save the dictater having to spell out the words unnecessarily. This is especially useful with highly technical terms which occur quite frequently, since all the employees in a typing centre are required to type the work of all the dictaters in the various departments of the organization.

Therefore, it is important not to rely on a typist to spell difficult sections of letters containing words which are unfamiliar because of their specialist nature. Nor is it good policy to leave her high and dry with obscure addresses which she may never have heard before and has no immediate means of checking as they come over her earphone. It involves little extra effort to the dictater to spell names and words which have several varying forms of spelling, rather than to leave the typist to guess, perhaps wrongly, thus involving retyping.

A word should not be spelled out without first giving the typist an idea of what it sounds like. If she hears a number of disembodied letters dictated without any knowledge of the whole word, she might be very confused. The correct procedure, therefore, is to announce the word followed by 'Typist please – I spell –. There should thus be no need for the typist to try her luck in spelling the doubtful word when she hears it and even if she is only a few words behind the dictater she has the satisfaction of knowing that he always makes a practice of spelling questionable words.

The method is to say the word first, then spell it, for example:

Clarke – typist please – I spell – CLARKE
Polyurethane – typist please – I spell – P for Papa –
OLYURETHA – N for November – E

When words have to be spelled out the dictater should use ordinary letters except when he meets confusable letters – those which sound very similar when spoken. Much more accuracy in interpretation can be achieved by using the phonetic alphabet. It does not matter which of the many versions a dictater may adopt. Whether he uses C for Charlie or C for Cat is of little consequence so long as he makes his meaning clear and the typist knows which letter she should use.

The following letters are among those which can cause confusion: B, P, V, D, T, F, S, M and N. When confusion is considered possible, use the phonetic alphabet given below.

Where a dictater has to spell out long words it will be to his advantage, and subsequently to the advantage of the audio typist, if he spells in groups or syllables as this makes for greater clarity. If two or more consecutive words have to be spelled then each one should be spelled immediately after saying it.

It is a useful habit for the dictater to adopt when he dictates initials or single letters as used in reference numbers, to use the phonetic alphabet, thereby eliminating chance. Long reference numbers are often the cause of confusion and, if not correctly indicated in correspondence, they can lead to long delays in response.

Below is the official phonetic alphabet as used by NATO, police forces and international air traffic control:

A	Alpha	J	Juliet	S	Sierra
B	Bravo	K	Kilo	T	Tango
C	Charlie	L	Lima	U	Uniform
D	Delta	M	Mike	V	Victor
E	Echo	N	November	W	Whisky
F	Foxtrot	O	Oscar	X	X-ray
G	Golf	P	Papa	Y	Yankee
H	Hotel	Q	Quebec	Z	Zulu
I	India	R	Romeo		

It is therefore important to remember that the typist is likely to have a Glossary containing:

- unusual words in common use in that organization;
- names and addresses in frequent use;
- any other information which will save the dictater having to spell out words.

Whenever there appears room for doubt regarding the correct spelling of a word or name, please spell.

Addresses are often the most unfamiliar part of the dictation to the typist, so make sure that she is not left in any doubt.

Method

A summary of the best method is therefore:

1   Say the word first, then spell it.
2   If words have to be spelled out, use ordinary letters except in the case of confusable letters, when the phonetic alphabet should be used.
3   Spell out in groups or syllables to make it more clear to the typist.
4   If two or more consecutive words need spelling, spell each one immediately after dictating it.
5   Always use the phonetic alphabet when dictating initials of names or single letters as in a reference.

Capital letters

During any dictation session a dictater may require a word or a series of words to be typed in capital letters in order to secure additional emphasis for them. To a lesser degree he may require only the initial letter of a word, or series of words to bear the capital. In both cases, it is necessary to inform the audio typist of the intention before she actually types the word or words.

Certain words are automatically written with an initial capital letter and the typist will know where to put these. The following therefore never need an instruction:

- proper nouns
- people's names
- months
- place names
- days
- company names

The method to use to indicate initial or full capital letters to the typist is:

1   Initial capitals.
'Our comprehensive – typist please – initial capital G – Glossary is of great assistance.'
2   Full capitals.
'Typist please – full capitals – USE PLEASE AND THANK YOU – end of full capitals – when dictating.'

In the case of an initial capital letter it must be remembered to give the required letter before dictating the word.

10 Punctuation principles

Correct punctuation is necessary for a proper understanding by the reader of what the writer or dictater wants to say. Many able writers claim with some truth that punctuation is nowadays becoming a neglected art. It is obvious that a failure to use punctuation rightly can confuse and irritate the reader. It is equally true that a well constructed sentence can often convey the sense of what is meant even though there are no punctuation marks, but such a sentence must be short and to the point.

Any person who is writing and dictating must bear in mind that, while he is fully aware of what he is trying to say, the person who is receiving his communication may be quite unfamiliar with it. A good rule for all composers is to remember that the recipient is not a thought reader and that, therefore, anything placed before him must be couched in simple and, where possible, brief terms. Correct punctuation therefore helps to convey the message clearly and simply. Messy punctuation can, on the other hand, prove confusing and even misleading. The same applies to fussy overpunctuation. There must be moderation. The indiscriminate use of commas, semicolons and the rest as though liberally sprinkled from a pepper pot can change the whole sense of a message and leave the reader bewildered. In short, simplicity should always be the aim. Therefore, remember:

1 Keep your sentences short.
2 Correct punctuation helps the reader to understand the content.
3 Do not overpunctuate.
4 Simplicity should always be the aim.

For the dictater who has to keep in mind the fact that he is producing matter for an audio typist it is imperative that he should remember that, unlike the shorthand typist seated at the other end of his desk, she does not have the advantage of seeing the piece of correspondence at the time of transcribing and, therefore, has no idea of the sequence of the text. It is too

Quick-draw punctuation

much to expect her to listen first and then go back to the beginning because, apart from this being a gross waste of time, it does not follow that she would be able to absorb and remember the whole sense and sequence of the letter to the extent of being able to punctuate correctly as intended by the dictater.

There are of course dictaters whose tones are of such quality that the appropriate punctuation symbol is implicit in their voices because they have paused, or their voice scale has lowered, just where necessary. These dictaters, however, are few and far between. In the general run it is very helpful for the dictater to follow the practice common to newspaper reporters who are dictating perhaps from a call box remote from the office and who, in the course of the dictation, put in the commas, hyphens, full stops, etc. It saves time and prevents confusion at the receiving end.

It would be a useful exercise for the dictater sometimes to put on the earphones normally found on the ears of the audio typist and listen to his own unpunctuated dictation. It might be a revelation to him of his own lack of understanding of the problem he creates! He might also realize how his various inflections suggesting a punctuation mark (but not necessarily indicating which) can lead the unsuspecting typist up the literary garden path.

As stated, the goal of punctuation is clarity, enabling the reader to understand at first glance and without undue mental strain the purport of the message. The symbols of punctuation comprise a series of stops or signs inserted to show the grammatical relationship of the words used, or to give emphasis to them. Some signs, such as the full stop and the comma, denote the length of a pause. Others, like the question mark, can be denoted by the inflexion of the voice, while signs for quotations and parenthesis serve to bring external matter into the basic text. The full stop and the comma are the most essential weapons in the armoury of the average composer of written matter and their sensible use can provide much of what is necessary to achieve simplicity and competence.

This chapter is designed to offer helpful advice to the communicator who, as a matter of business practice, wants his communications to be understood and appreciated without their having to be read twice over. Points to observe:

1   The audio typist does not listen to the dictation prior to typing, therefore do not rely on the typist to punctuate for you.
2   Never rely on your intonation of voice as an indication of punctuation as this could only, at best, allow guesswork on the part of the typist.

A LIST OF PROGRAMME HEADINGS IS ENCLOSED PLEASE TELEPHONE IF YOU REQUIRE ADDITIONAL INFORMATION

The full stop

The full stop is the most essential symbol in all writing, though there are times when a colon or semi-colon would be better employed. However, if the dictater habitually uses short sentences, as he is well advised to, his text will contain relatively many full stops, and be all the clearer as a result.

The comma

The comma marks the shortest pause. It helps to convey the meaning of the sentence and its correct use can only be acquired by common sense, reading

IF YOU WISH TO SHOOT THE ATTENDANT WILL BE GLAD TO LOAD YOUR GUN

and practice. Care must be exercised to avoid the peppering of matter with commas. This can be done by the use of short sentences, because a long sentence sprinkled with commas can produce confusion and misunderstanding.

It is incorrect to use a comma between two independent sentences not linked by a conjunction. The usual practice here is to use a heavier stop, usually a semi-colon, but preferably a full stop. Thus, again, we have the short sentence.

MY SECRETARY LIKES THE OPEN PLAN OFFICE NO DOUBT PLANTS ARE PREFERABLE TO PAINTED WALLS

The semi-colon

The semi-colon marks a pause less powerful than the full stop, and is rarely necessary in business correspondence if it is appropriately clipped by means of the use of short sentences. There are times, however, when the use of the semi-colon can mark a more decisive break in the sense of the communication than is the case when a comma is used. It is stronger than a comma but tends to snap the continuity, and care should be exercised in its use. It might well be regarded as a 'slow down' signal.

HERE IS A LIST OF CHIEF LETTER WRITING VICES VAGUE-NESS LONGWINDEDNESS AND INACCURACY

The colon

This is a useful symbol, though its systematic use for pause value is declining. It is generally agreed, however, that it still has its uses as something less than a full stop and more than a semi-colon. It is useful when preceding an explanation or introducing a list or series, for example: 'The goods enclosed consist of: ...'.

The colon can be followed by a dash if a list or series follows.

IT CANNOT BE DENIED PERHAPS IT MAY EVEN BE THAT BLACK IS NOT WHITE

Parentheses

The use of parentheses (brackets) is to introduce an additional piece of information into a sentence that is normally complete without it. The parenthesis is a useful adjunct in writing but needs to be employed sparingly lest too many features may be introduced into a sentence thus causing it to be cumbersome and confusing. Properly used it can help to convey a clear meaning; abused it leads to misunderstanding.

It is always good policy to repeat some features of a letter to secure greater emphasis and clarity, such as:

Our price is £200 (two hundred pounds)

or as the military sometimes have it:

You will not (repeat, not) proceed with Plan B

Here the brackets are an aid to the continuity of the message as well as giving emphasis, and can be used with confidence.

HE IS AN EXCEPTIONAL SALESMAN WHO COULD SELL YOU YOUR OWN SHOES AND WHAT IS MORE YOU WOULD PROBABLY WANT TO BUY THEM

The hyphen

A teacher asked a small boy, 'Why do we use a hyphen to join words such as bird-cage?' and the boy innocently replied, 'For the bird to perch on.' Many modern writers use the hyphen unnecessarily to join up entirely separate words which are entitled to stand up on their own. There are purists who detest the hyphen and go to the extreme length of not using it at all; this can lead to clumsy looking words, especially those where there is a double vowel. For example, a hyphen is preferred in words such as re-emphasize and re-establish.

The hyphen is unnecessary with two consonants such as in dissatisfaction, dissemination, disservice, dissimilar or dissociate.

Where it is necessary to use a hyphen at the end of a line, care should be exercised to make sure that the split is made at the correct break: not unself-conscious but un-selfconscious.

The modern trend is to employ solid or separate words in preference to the use of the hyphen, but it is useful as a link joining two adjectives describing a noun as in: a first-class service, a long-winded letter − or after certain prefixes, such as in: ex-chairman, post-industrial − or in such combinations of words as: mother-in-law, son-in-law, etc, and in numerals: twenty-three, forty-six, etc.

Proper names such as Great Britain, New England, New Brunswick are not hyphenated, but such combinations as Anglo-Asian and Franco-German are.

Nouns that are made up from two other nouns, such as bath and room, farm and hand, combine to make one word: bathroom and farmhand respectively. The easiest way to recognize the way to write such combinations is to pronounce them. If the stress or accent is thrown more on one part of the word than the other it is the more likely to be a single word.

THE GOODS WERE PROMISED TWO MONTHS AGO WHEN CAN WE EXPECT DELIVERY

The question mark

Question marks are necessary only at the end of direct questions. Indirect questions do not require them. 'Where did you spend your holiday?' demands a question mark, but 'I am writing to ask where you spent your holiday' does not. Politeness requires a question mark if the query is: 'Will you please let me know when you will arrive?' though it is not necessary.

THE MANAGER SAID YOU ARE FIRED

Quotation marks

It is an interesting reflection that quotation marks (inverted commas) are not used in the Bible which some people consider to be the best piece of all literature; nor are they used in the literature of the eighteenth century. They can therefore be truly described as a rather modern innovation. But they have their uses and the business correspondence of today sometimes needs the use of inverted commas, though the writer should be careful to avoid an overindulgence in them. It would be correct to quote:

I see that you have said: 'There can be no going back on my previous declaration on this point' but may I urge....

But it might be better to rephrase the letter:

I note what you say in your previous declaration but....

Inverted commas are a useful device to quote slang or facetious matter, thus making it clear to the reader that the writer says what he is saying with tongue in cheek, but most business correspondence makes the use of inverted commas a rare requirement.

Punctuation at the end of a quotation

There has been much debate on whether punctuation marks should be placed before or after the inverted commas that close a quotation. Generally, if a quotation stands alone, the full point or comma should be placed within the quotation marks, but if the quotation forms only part of a wider sentence, the punctuation should fall outside the quotation marks – as in this book. In America, however, all full stops and commas fall inside the quotation marks.

Other punctuation marks are placed inside or outside the closing quotation mark according to sense. Double quotation marks should be used for the main quotation; single quotes only for a quotation within the main quotation – this is because single quotes can be mistaken for apostrophes.

DEAR MR BROWN AT LAST THE COOPER CONTRACT IS IN THE BAG

The exclamation mark

The exclamation mark is what it is denoted to be, an exclamation mark. It should be used sparingly and only when an exclamation has been interposed into the text. Some writers tend to use the exclamation mark at the end of almost every sentence, which is quite wrong as very few sentences are exclamations. In deciding the appropriateness of the use of the exclamation mark think of the meaning of the verb 'to exclaim'. It is, in effect, 'to cry out' and it would be legitimate to use it where one has made an exclamation such as 'Oh yeah!' It is also not unusual to find it where the writer appears to be expressing a doubt about an assertion such as: 'A call by a commercial traveller (he calls himself a sales representative!).'

Capital letters

There is a tendency nowadays for the 'arty' to use few, if any, capital letters and violate every canon of standard written English. Advertisers – many of them big spenders in the national Press and on television – are among the guilty in the misuse, or lack of use, of capital letters. However, having said this, it must be confessed that such things are to some extent a matter of personal usage and of fashion. Perhaps this fashion will soon give way to another.

Apart from their standard use in proper names and at the start of sentences, capital letters can sometimes be used with the aim of giving added emphasis in typewriting where italic type would be used in a book. A word typed in its entirety in capitals can serve a very useful purpose.

Brackets, inverted commas and underlining

Since the audio typist does not have personal contact with the dictater but listens to his recording through a pair of stethoscope earphones, she needs to receive clear instructions regarding the content of the letter before she starts to type it so as to leave sufficient spaces for such essentials as brackets or inverted commas.

A measure of standardization in an office in which all who dictate adopt the same method is a useful labour-saving device which makes it less likely for the audio typist to make a mistake. A fully trained and competent girl is usually only a few words behind the dictater. Thus, if instructions are left to come after the words to which they refer, it may well be too late. In all probability the typist, being unaware at the moment of typing that they are intended, may not have left the necessary space for symbols.

The correct method of imparting the necessary instruction in this respect is as follows.

1 *Brackets.*
   I shall be there – *bracket* – barring any holdups – *close bracket* – at ten o'clock.
2 *Quotes.*
   The bus conductor said – *quote* – only room for one more passenger – *close quote.*

When it becomes necessary to underline any words or even whole sentences there is no need to inform the typist before dictating the content as it will be easy for her to bring her carriage back to the beginning of the required underlining. But always remember, as mentioned in the previous pages, to take the precaution of preceding the instruction with the words, 'Typist please –'

Headings which the dictater desires underlined should, of course, be mentioned after dictating the matter. Such instruction, however, is dependent upon the policy and style of the individual company to which every member of the staff conforms. Many organizations have a standard policy always to underline headings. If this is so, it is not necessary to instruct the typist about it, but in relation to other underlinings it is essential to ensure that the typist is properly instructed.

In the question of underlining text matter it is wise to reserve this for really important sections of the communication. Excessive underlining produces imbalance in the ratio of importance and loses the emphasis which it is intended to convey.

The method to follow is:

1   Make sure the opening bracket or inverted comma is announced before the content is dictated.
2   The alternative instruction to inverted comma is *quote*.
3   Underlining needs no pre-indication.
4   An excess of underlining should be avoided.

11 Money and figures

Any dictater who plunges into a dictation session which contains sets of figures or money and who does not follow a strict pattern of instruction is inviting trouble because there are many and varied pitfalls. These can be avoided only if the right approach is used.

Dictation pitfalls

Consider first dictation involving the typing of amounts of money. It is essential to dictate the currency symbol before mentioning the sum. It is easy for the audio typist to follow dictation in its chronological order and type '100,000 pounds' where '£100,000' is intended.

The correct method is to dictate:

This will be invoiced at £ sterling 30 per tonne.

By giving the '£' sterling introduction in this manner the typist is forewarned about the symbol.

If, however, the dictater is working on weights there is no need to do this as this always comes after the figure. For example:

The birthweight of the baby was 3.5 kg.

Great care needs to be taken in the dictation of figures lest, by dictating at too great a speed, the typist may miss out a vital figure and thereby make nonsense of the communication. When long numbers, such as serial or reference numbers, need to be dictated it is helpful to the typist to dictate figures in single digits. Instead of saying hundreds, thousands and millions, it is less likely to cause confusion if the comma is used.

The correct method of dictating a sum such as £50,575,123 is:

£ sterling 50 space (or comma) 575 space (comma) 123.

In some cases numbers need to be typed in words and in others the dictater will want them to be shown in figures. In commercial correspondence, the general rule is that numbers up to and including ten will be written out in words. Above this, figures will be used except where a number opens a sentence.

Below are some examples showing the correct method:

- There was an audience of 250 people.
- We have sent you four reminders in the last two months.
- Four tons at £45 per ton.
- Nearly 50 years ago.
- Our lunch appointment was at 1230.
- Four 2-gallon containers.

There will, of course, be some exceptions to the rule of typing out numbers but in every case the dictater must give clear instructions, otherwise the work may have to be returned for retyping.

The correct instruction should be: 'In words' or 'In figures'.

12 List of words which sound similar

Few languages have a more difficult system of spelling than English. There are many words in frequent use which are confusing to the audio typist because, though they have more than one meaning, they are pronounced in the same way (or seem to be). It has been emphasized that spelling is largely the responsibility of the dictater where there is any element of doubt, and the following words have been selected (there are many more) to illustrate the point.

Accede	Exceed	Close	Close
Accent	Ascent	Compliment	Complement
	Assent	Confident	Confidant
Accept	Except	Corps	Core
Adapt	Adopt		Corpse
Addition	Edition	Counsel	Council
Advice	Advise	Course	Coarse
Affect	Effect	Cue	Queue
Allusion	Illusion	Currant	Current
Bare	Bear	Dependant	Dependent
Base	Bass	Descendent	Descendant
Boarder	Border	Device	Devise
Borough	Burrow	Dictator	Dictater
Brake	Break	Discreet	Discrete
Cession	Session	Divers	Diverse
Choir	Quire	Draft	Draught
Choler	Collar	Elusive	Illusive
	Colour	Ensure	Insure
Cite	Site	Envelop	Envelope
	Sight	Era	Error
Errand	Errant	Principle	Principal
Flair	Flare	Prophecy	Prophesy

Formerly	Formally	Right	Rite
Idol	Idle	Seize	Cease
Illicit	Elicit	Serial	Cereal
Immanent	Imminent	Spacious	Specious
Led	Lead	Stationary	Stationery
Lesser	Lessor	Straitened	Straightened
Licence	License	Sweet	Suite
Lose	Loose	Tear	Tare
Minor	Miner		Tier
Monetary	Monitory	Tenor	Tenure
Peak	Pique	Tortuous	Tortious
Pendant	Pendent	Veracity	Voracity
Personal	Personnel	Waist	Waste
Place	Plaice	Waiver	Waver
Populous	Populace	Where	Wear
Practice	Practise		Ware
Precedence	Precedents	Write	Wright

PART III

SPECIMEN DICTATING PROCEDURES

13 Business Letters

Business letters and memoranda (both internal and external) and draft reports lend themselves admirably to the process of dictation, and the relaxed dictater finds it easy to produce a smooth and readable end result. Yet this occurs only when he has familiarized himself with the equipment and can handle it with the same automatic ease with which he manipulates the controls of his car. Practice makes perfect and a user who becomes thoroughly accustomed to his instrument can concentrate his mind on the construction of the phrases in the matter in hand.

The internal memo, which has a very limited circulation within the firm, should not involve much strain in the matter of its construction. So long as it conveys clearly what the writer wants to say it will serve its purpose. The business letter, however, is rather different in that it conveys to people outside the firm something of the character, prestige and business capacity of those within it. The business letter, therefore, requires a greater measure of concentration and care in its construction, and it is here that the dictater needs to have his mind free from thoughts of the 'automatic machine' which lies before him.

The following examples show how different kinds of letters are structured and 'laid out' by the dictater.

Example 1

Good morning typist – this is J D Brown, Chief Buyer, telephone extension number 473.

    I require a letter please – medium length – top copy and three carbon copies. Our reference number W Whisky – B Bravo – stroke – J Juliet – D Delta – B Bravo – stroke – 1093 – W Whisky – B Bravo. … The letter is to go to:
John Smith & Co Ltd
Heswall House – *I spell – capital H – E – S – for Sierra – W – A – double L*
Barnacle Road – *I spell – capital B – A – R – N for November – A – C – L – E*
London NW3
Letter commences:
Dear Sirs – *comma – Typist please – centre heading – underlined –* Re *capital W* – Waste *– hyphen –* Bins.
Will you please send us a quotation for – *typist please – in figures –* 76 – *open bracket – (in words –* seventy-six *– close bracket)* of your *capitals* A *– stop –* B *– stop –* C *– stop –* one nine waste *hyphen* bins and also indicate how soon we may expect delivery after the placing of a firm order – *question mark – new paragraph.*
We are also interested in bins of a similar size – *comma –* weight and capacity as mentioned in your recent advertisement – *full stop –* Can you let us have the prices of each type – *comma –* singly and by the gross – *question mark.*
Letter ends – Yours faithfully – *comma.*
J D Brown
Chief Buyer
Typist please – copies to go to Mr James in Publicity and Mr Hall in Sales – Thank you.

WB/JDB/1093/WB
John Smith & Co Ltd
Heswall House
Barnacle Road
London NW3

Date

Dear Sirs,

Re Waste-bins

Will you please send us a quotation for 76 (seventy-six) of your A.B.C.
19 waste-bins and also indicate how soon we may expect delivery after
the placing of a firm order?

We are also interested in bins of a similar size, weight and capacity as
mentioned in your recent advertisement. Can you let us have the prices
of each type, singly and by the gross?

Yours faithfully,

J D Brown
Chief Buyer

Example 2

*Good morning typist – Mr S A Smith speaking – Personnel Manager – telephone
extension number 123*
*Would you please type a medium sized letter – one top copy, one copy – on size A4
paper. The letter is to go to:*
Miss M – *for Mike* – E Johnson
The Old Mill
Wharf Road – *I spell – capital W – h – a – r – f for Foxtrot*
Biddlesea – *I spell – capital B – i – double d – l – e –s – e – a*
Gloucestershire
Letter commences:
Dear Miss Johnson – *comma – Typist please – centre heading – underlined – Re
capital Y* – Your application form.
Thank you for your letter and completed form of application for the post of
– *typist please – capital S* – Secretary to our – *capital G* – General – *capital M*
– Manager – *full stop – new paragraph.*
The details you supply regarding yourself suggest that you may possess the
qualifications and experience required – *full stop* – I would like – *comma* –
therefore – *comma* – to pursue the matter further with you – *full stop* – *new
paragraph.*
Would it be possible for you to call on me for interview at – *comma* say –
comma – 1100 next Tuesday – *question mark* – If so – *comma* – please
telephone your confirmation of this arrangement – *full stop.*

Signed

Yours sincerely – *comma*

Thank you typist

SAS/AB
Miss M E Johnson
The Old Mill
Wharf Road
Biddlesea
Gloucestershire   Date
Dear Miss Johnson,

Re Your application form

Thank you for your letter and completed form of application for the post
of Secretary to our General Manager.

The details you supply regarding yourself suggest that you may possess the qualifications and experience required. I would like, therefore,
to pursue the matter further with you.

Would it be possible for you to call on me for interview at, say, 11 a.m.
next Tuesday? If so, please telephone your confirmation of this
arrangement.

Yours sincerely,
S A Smith
Personnel Manager

Example 3

Good afternoon typist – this is Arthur Brown, General Manager, telephone number 46.
This is a letter please with two carbon copies – one for each file – no special layout.
Reference number A for Alpha – B for Bravo – stroke – figures 34 – capital B – stroke – capitals C – stop – D – stop.
Letter to be sent to:
G – *stop* – E – *stop* – Armstrong Esquire
Export Manager
Blaides – *I spell* – *capital* B – l – a – i – d *for Delta* – e – s and Jones Ltd
Saltash House
Middletown
Letter begins:
Dear Mr Armstrong – *comma* –*Typist please* – *centre heading* – *underlined* –Re
Your order number – *capitals* GE *space* 1234

Thank you for your order number *capitals* GE *space* 1234 of the 12th August for one gross of our special containers – *open bracket* – our catalogue number 34 – *capital* B – *close bracket* – at – *typist please* – *in words* – thirty-six pence each – *full stop* – *new paragraph.*

These have now been completed and are available for dispatch – *full stop* – In your order you stated that you might want them delivered to your Middlesbrough depot but that you would let me know later whether this was so – *full stop* – *new paragraph.*

If you would kindly let me know where to send them – *comma* – they will be posted on the day I hear from you – *full stop*
Yours sincerely *comma* – *end of letter* – *thank you.*

AB/34B/C.D.
G. E. Armstrong Esq
Export Manager
Blaides & Jones Ltd
Saltash House
Middletown

Date

Dear Mr Armstrong,

Re Your order number GE 1234

Thank you for your order number GE 1234 of the 12th August for one gross of our special containers (our catalogue number 34B) at thirty-six pence each.

These have now been completed and are available for dispatch. In your order you stated that you might want them delivered to your Middlesbrough depot but that you would let me know later whether this was so.

If you would kindly let me know where to send them, they will be posted on the day I hear from you.

Yours sincerely,

Arthur Brown
General Manager

14 The internal memo

The internal memo, whether it is short or long, should convey quite clearly the message the sender intends. Normally an internal memo should be short unless the subject matter is particularly complex. Here are examples of internal memos in suitable form.

Good morning typist, I require a memo to be sent to the Export Manager from Mr Jones, General Manager, one copy for the file.
Memo begins:
Messrs Brown and Thompson – *I spell* – *capital* T – h – o – m *for Mike* – p *for Papa* – s – o – n *for November* – tell me that there has been a delay in the dispatch by us of their order of 10 September – *open bracket* – their reference – *capitals* OUS – *figures 42* – *dash* – our reference – *capitals* – AGB – *stroke* – 76 – *stroke* – 2 – *close bracket* – *full stop* – Is there any reason for this – *question mark* – Please let me know and also inform me what the prospects are of a speedy satisfaction of this valued customer – *full stop* – *end of memo* – *thank you.*

Memo from General Manager to Export Manager

Messrs Brown and Thompson tell me that there has been a delay in the dispatch by us of their order of 10 September (their ref. OUS 42 – our ref. AGB/76/2). Is there any reason for this? Please let me know and also inform me what the prospects are of a speedy satisfaction of this valued customer.

Good afternoon – J Brown – Public Relations Department – extension 44 – Please type a memo with six copies to the Borough Engineer – one copy to go on file – five copies to go to Mr A Smith – Mr B Jones – Mr C Green – Mr D Taylor – Mr E Harris – names of the recipients to be typed in red
Memo starts:
The local – *capital P* – Press are insistent upon information regarding the delays in the thorough cleansing of – *capital A* – Applegate – *capital S* – Street – *full stop* – The suggestion is that there has been tardy supervision of the street cleaners with the result that rubbish is allowed to accumulate to such an extent that there are piles of it which are reaching such proportions that they are impeding passage on the pavements – *exclamation mark* – *new paragraph* – Will you please let me have as much information on this subject as you possibly can – *comma* – and as soon as you can – *comma* – because delay in satisfying the – *capital P* – Press in a matter of this kind reflects badly on our efficiency – *full stop* – *signed* – J Brown – PRO – *Thank you typist*

PRO to Borough Engineer

The local Press are insistent upon information regarding the delays in the thorough cleansing of Applegate Street. The suggestion is that there has been tardy supervision of the street cleaners with the result that rubbish is allowed to accumulate to such an extent that there are

piles of it which are reaching such proportions that they are impeding
passage on the pavements!

Will you please let me have as much information on this subject as you
possibly can, and as soon as you can, because delay in satisfying the
Press in a matter of this kind reflects badly on our efficiency.

J Brown PRO

*Good morning Mary, W Brown, Dept G here. I require a memo – one copy – to
Mr Wallace, Dept A.*
Please type the following:
I understand that there has been a delay in the completion of certain orders
for the supply of – *typist please* – *full capitals for the next two words* –
GALVANISED WASHERS – *full stop* – Why – *question mark* – Will you
please let me have details of the cause of any hold – *hyphen* – ups – *full stop* –
If – *comma* – in fact – *comma* – the trouble is internal – *comma* – please give
the reasons and your suggestions for overcoming the difficulties – *full stop* –
end of memo – *thank you*

W Brown, Dept G to Mr Wallace, Dept A

I understand that there has been a delay in the completion of certain
orders for the supply of GALVANISED WASHERS. Why? Will you please
let me have details of the cause of any hold-ups. If, in fact, the trouble
is internal, please give the reasons and your suggestions for overcoming the difficulties.

W Brown, Dept G

*This is A B C Brown, Housing Manager, extension 769. Good morning typist.
This is a fairly long memorandum. I require four copies – one for central file – the
rest to go to the Town Clerk, the Borough Architect, and the Borough Treasurer
I require a centre heading with two lines – first line – Reconstruction and Repair
of Premises in – last line – quote – Limekiln Lane – close quote*
Memorandum begins:
The Housing Committee has decided to recommend to the Council that the
six cottages numbers – *typist please* – *in figures* – 1 to 6 *open bracket inclusive*
– *close bracket* – in Limekiln Lane be examined with a view to reconstruction
– *open bracket* – where necessary – *close bracket* – and extensive repair and
improvement – *full stop* – Improvement grants are available in respect of
some of the proposed work – *full stop* – The proposals are tentative at the
moment and largely depend on – *colon* – *Typist please* – *there will now be four
small sub-paragraphs* – *I require these to be numbered and indented four spaces to
the right*

One – A decision whether the premises are repairable at all – *full stop* –
Two – Whether they are repairable at a reasonable outlay –*full stop* –
Three – If numbers – *typist please* – *in figures* – one and six – *comma* – which it
is obvious are in a much worse state than the remainder of the terrace –
comma – have to be demolished – *comma* – the flank walls remaining can be
built up to ensure the stability of the four remaining cottages to make the
task of restoration and modernisation worth while – *full stop*
Four – An estimate of the cost – *comma* – to be provided by you – *full stop* –
new paragraph – *also end of the sub-sections* – Will you please have a survey
made with these points in mind –*question mark* – It would be appreciated if
you will kindly report as soon as possible – *comma* – conveying your ideas
of what can and can not be done with these premises and indicating whether
– *comma* – in your opinion – *comma* – any scheme for the restoration of all or
part of the terrace is a viable proposition – *full stop* – In the event of your
being satisfied that a scheme is in fact viable and reasonable will you please
prepare plans and estimates to indicate to the Committee what – *comma* – in
your considered opinion – *comma* – can and should be done and an
indication of the likely cost – *full stop* – *new paragraph* –It would be helpful
also if you could indicate whether – *comma* – in the event of any works
being proceeded with – *comma* – it would be necessary to re – *hyphen* –
house any of the tenants in temporary accommodation during the period of
the works – *full stop* – *new paragraph* – The chairman of the Committee has
told me that he regards the condition of – *typist* – *in figures* – one to six
Limekiln Lane as a matter of some urgency – *full stop* – *end of memorandum* –
signed A B C Brown – *comma* – Housing Manager – *thank you*

Memorandum from Housing Manager

Copies for information to:
Town Clerk
Borough Architect
Borough Treasurer

Reconstruction and Repair of Premises in "Limekiln Lane"

The Housing Committee has decided to recommend to the Council that
the six cottages numbers 1 to 6 (inclusive) in Limekiln Lane be examined with a view to reconstruction (where necessary) and extensive
repair and improvement. Improvement grants are available in respect
of some of the proposed work. The proposals are tentative at the
moment and largely depend on:

1 A decision whether the premises are repairable at all.
2 Whether they are repairable at a reasonable outlay.

3   If numbers 1 and 6, which it is obvious are in a much worse state than the remainder of the terrace, have to be demolished, the flank walls remaining can be built up to ensure the stability of the four remaining cottages to make the task of restoration and modernisation worth while.

4   An estimate of the cost, to be provided by you.

Will you please have a survey made with these points in mind? It would be appreciated if you will kindly report as soon as possible, conveying your ideas of what can and can not be done with these premises and indicating whether, in your opinion, any scheme for the restoration of all or part of the terrace is a viable proposition. In the event of your being satisfied that a scheme is in fact viable and reasonable will you please prepare plans and estimates to indicate to the Committee what, in your considered opinion, can and should be done and an indication of the likely cost.

It would be helpful also if you could indicate whether, in the event of any works being proceeded with, it would be necessary to re-house any of the tenants in temporary accommodation during the period of the works.

The Chairman of the Committee has told me that he regards the condition of 1 to 6 Limekiln Lane as a matter of some urgency.

A B C Brown,
Housing Manager

15 The draft report

It sometimes happens that an executive is uncertain as to what should be the content of a report or memo and how it should be expressed. In such cases he considers it useful to get his views on to paper in a rough and preliminary form in order that he can 'get his mind organized'. He thus dictates his ideas, not necessarily in the order in which they should appear in the finished product but merely as an *aide-memoire* when he comes to polish the final draft. The first draft may, therefore, appear to be a jumble of unconnected comments and could read something like the following:

Good morning Mary. This will be a draft. Will you please type this IN DOUBLE SPACING – with two extra copies for correction – to be sent to all Executives and Departmental Heads – heading to read – Reorganization of Departments *– will you underline that please*

The draft reads as follows:

It has become evident that in order to increase efficiency a major reorganization of departments will have to be considered *– full stop –* To do this there are many factors which must be brought into mind *– comma –* such as *– colon –* Mary *– please start a new line here for each item –* 1 The effect on existing personnel *–* 2 Whether any redundancies can be absorbed into other departments which may be built up to undertake wider responsibility *– question mark –* 3 If the merging of any departments can be shown to be possible and effective *– question mark –* 4 Are there any activities which can be discarded in order to produce greater efficiency and higher productivity in other lines *– question mark –* 5 Are we satisfied that our existing organization is one hundred per cent efficient and adequate to the requirements of our business *– question mark –* 6 Does our sales staff do all that we desire of it *– question mark –* 7 Should it be increased or reduced *– question mark –* 8 Are there any factors that militate against the successful conduct of our business *– question mark –* 9 Are there any items of our machinery that need renewal or can we be confident that a complete reorganization of the various departments to give a smoother flow of production *– open bracket –* and a reduction in walking time by operatives from machine to machine – *close bracket* – is necessary – *question mark* – 10 Are there any means of speeding production and – *oblique* – or – producing an even better finished product in less time – *question mark* – *new paragraph* – These are questions which every executive in the Company is asked to look at very seriously – *full stop* – *new paragraph* – I am proposing to call a conference of departmental heads to discuss as freely as may be the various factors which may be militating against our complete efficiency and I would welcome any suggestions which may be a helpful source of discussion – *full stop* – *new paragraph* – In the meantime please let me have a report on the circumstances obtaining in your own department together with any ideas you may have for any improvement – *full stop* – No matter how outlandish your ideas may seem I want to have them –*full stop* – signed J Robertson – Managing Director

To all Executives and Departmental Heads
Reorganization of Departments

It has become evident that in order to increase efficiency a major reorganization of departments will have to be considered. To do this there are many factors which must be brought into mind, such as:

1   The effect on existing personnel
2   Whether any redundancies can be absorbed into other departments which may be built up to undertake wider responsibility?
3   If the merging of any departments can be shown to be possible and effective?
4   Are there any activities which can be discarded in order to produce greater efficiency and higher productivity in other lines?
5   Are we satisfied that our existing organization is one hundred per cent efficient and adequate to the requirements of our business?
6   Does our sales staff do all that we desire of it?
7   Should it be increased or reduced?
8   Are there any factors that militate against the successful conduct of our business?
9   Are there any items of our machinery that need renewal or can we be confident that a complete reorganization of the various departments to give a smoother flow of production (and a reduction in walking time by operatives from machine to machine) is necessary?
10 Are there any means of speeding production and/or producing an even better finished product in less time?

These are questions which every executive in the Company is asked to look at very seriously.

I am proposing to call a conference of departmental heads to discuss as freely as may be the various factors which may be militating against our complete efficiency and I would welcome any suggestions which may be a helpful source of discussion.

In the meantime please let me have a report on the circumstances obtaining in your own department together with any ideas you may have for any improvement. No matter how outlandish your ideas may seem I want to have them.

J. Robertson
Managing Director

The draft report

16 The finished report with special layout instructions

It can quite often be the case that an audio typist has greater difficulty with the instructions attached to a piece of dictation than with the typing as such. This is particularly true when the dictation is not only comparatively lengthy but when its layout on the page is both complex and important. In such circumstances the need to give full and clear instructions – and to give them in good time – is even more vital than with items where a typist could be relied upon, at least to some extent, to follow a standard format or to use her initiative.

Good afternoon Mary, thank you for the draft you typed – I have now amended this so would you please type the final. I suggest that we have one top copy and two copies – the top copy to be photocopied and sent to each Departmental Head and Executive. Since the following ten subject headings are of the utmost importance I would like these to be typed in full capitals – numbered instead of using small letters, and underlined. Will you leave four to six spaces free at the beginning of each subject matter and, to give emphasis to the ten points, please box them in. This will be addressed to all Executive and Departmental Heads. The centre heading to be typed in full capitals as follows:
Possible Reorganization to increase Efficiency and Productivity – It would appear that there has been a falling off in productivity during the last quarter and I am anxious to ascertain the cause and – *comma* – if possible – *comma* – to deal with it – *full stop*. To do this I would appreciate your full cooperation – *full stop* – *new paragraph* – I am proposing to call a conference of all – *Mary – in full capitals please* – Executives and Departmental Heads – *end full capitals* – in the near future to engage in an investigation in depth of the causes of our decline and to discover means of arresting it – *full stop* – By this means we can discuss as freely as possible the factors which may be militating against our complete efficiency and I shall welcome any suggestions you may have to offer – *full stop* – *new paragraph* – In the meantime will you please let me have a report on the circumstances obtaining in your depart-

ment together with any ideas you may have for any improvement – *full stop* – No matter how outlandish your ideas may appear to be I would still like to have them because they may make a contribution towards finding what we are seeking – *Mary please put a dash here* – greater efficiency – *comma* – better productivity and – *comma* – where it can be achieved – *comma* – reduced cost – *full stop* – *new paragraph* – As a guide I suggest we can look at the possibility of making a major reorganization of methods and even of departments – *full stop* – Questions which will bear on this subject will – *comma* – naturally – *comma* – include – *colon*

Mary, this is where the ten points start so leave enough space for the boxing in – and headings in capitals please

1 – *in full capitals* – Departments – *indent four spaces* – *in the next line* – The possible merging of two or more departments – *full stop* – 2 – *heading in caps* – Personnel – *next line* – The effect on existing personnel – *full stop* – 3 – *heading in caps* – Redundancy Absorption – Whether any prospective redundancies can be absorbed by other departments – *question mark* – 4 – *heading* – Company activities – *next line* – Are there any activities of the Company which are unprofitable and can be discarded in order to produce greater efficiency and a higher productivity in other and more remunerative lines – *question mark* – 5 – *heading* – Efficiency – *next line* – Are we satisfied that our existing organization is one hundred per cent – *Mary type per cent out in words* – efficient and truly adequate to the requirements of our business – *question mark* – 6 – *heading* – Sales staff – *next line* – Is our sales staff as effective as it might be –*question mark* – *open bracket* – Should it be increased – *comma* – reduced or only encouraged to a new display of energy – *question mark* – *close bracket* – 7 *heading* – Inter – *hyphen* – Company conduct – *next line* – Are there any factors that act against the successful conduct of our business – *open bracket* – restrictive practices – *comma* – indolence – *comma* – carelessness or anything else – *close bracket* – *question mark* – 8 – *heading* – Replacement of machinery – *next line* – Are there any items of our machinery that need renewal – *question mark* – 9 – *heading* – Improvement of production flow – *next line* Would the reorganization of any department – *open bracket* – even if it involves the transfer of machinery to new siting to give a smoother flow of production and a reduction of walking time by operatives from machine to machine – *close bracket* – be a help – *question mark* – 10 – *heading* – Improvement of finished goods – Are there any means of speeding production and – *oblique* – or producing an even better finished article in less time –*question mark* – *next paragraph* – You may have other points in mind which will help – *full stop* – Let me know them – *full stop* – In a major investigation of this kind nothing is too small to be considered – *full stop* – *new paragraph* – Let me make it clear – *comma* – I am not being critical of anybody – *full stop* – However – *comma* – I must know and this can only be achieved by informing me of your on – *hyphen* – the – *hyphen* – spot knowledge of our activities – *full stop* – *signed* – J Robertson

<u>To all Executives and Departmental Heads</u>

<u>POSSIBLE REORGANIZATION</u>
<u>TO INCREASE EFFICIENCY AND PRODUCTIVITY</u>

It would appear that there has been a falling off in productivity during the last quarter and I am anxious to ascertain the cause and, if possible, to deal with it. To do this I would appreciate your full cooperation.

I am proposing to call a conference of all EXECUTIVES AND DEPARTMENTAL HEADS in the near future to engage in an investigation in depth of the causes of our decline and to discover means of arresting it. By this means we can discuss as freely as possible the factors which may be militating against our complete efficiency and I shall welcome any suggestions you may have to offer.

In the meantime will you please let me have a report on the circumstances obtaining in your own department together with any ideas you may have for any improvement. No matter how outlandish your ideas may appear to be I would still like to have them because they may make a contribution towards finding what we are seeking – greater efficiency, better productivity and, where it can be achieved, reduced cost.

As a guide I suggest we can look at the possibility of making a major reorganization of methods and even of departments. Questions which will bear on this subject will, naturally, include those shown on the attached sheet [opposite].

You may have other points in mind which will help. Let me know them. In a major investigation of this kind nothing is too small to be considered.

Let me make it clear, I am not being critical of anybody. However, I must know and this can only be achieved by informing me of your on-the-spot knowledge of our activities.

J Robertson
<u>Managing Director</u>

1 <u>DEPARTMENTS</u>
The possible merging of two or more departments.

2 <u>PERSONNEL</u>
The effect on existing personnel.

3 <u>REDUNDANCY ABSORPTION</u>
Whether any prospective redundancies can be absorbed by other departments?

4 <u>COMPANY ACTIVITIES</u>
Are there any activities of the Company which are unprofitable and can be discarded in order to produce greater efficiency and a higher productivity in other and more remunerative lines?

5 <u>EFFICIENCY</u>
Are we satisfied that our existing organization is one hundred per cent efficient and truly adequate to the requirements of our business?

6 <u>SALES STAFF</u>
Is our sales staff as effective as it might be? (Should it be increased, reduced or only encouraged to a new display of energy?)

7 <u>INTER-COMPANY CONDUCT</u>
Are there any factors that act against the successful conduct of our business (restrictive practices, indolence, carelessness or anything else)?

8 <u>REPLACEMENT OF MACHINERY</u>
Are there any items of our machinery that need renewal?

9 <u>IMPROVEMENT OF PRODUCTION FLOW</u>
Would the reorganization of any department (even if it involves the transfer of machinery to new siting to give a smoother flow of production and a reduction of walking time by operatives from machine to machine) be a help?

10 <u>IMPROVEMENT OF FINISHED GOODS</u>
Are there any means of speeding production and/or producing an even better finished article in less time?

17 Tabular material

When it becomes necessary to dictate a small tabulation within the body of a letter, the dictater must first make sure that he has all relevant information on his desk before starting on the content of the columns. Below is an example of a letter which contains the kind of tabulation that can easily be dictated through any system:

Good afternoon typist, this is A Gordon, sales department, extension number 765. The following is a letter which will include a tabulation — I require three carbon copies. I will dictate the subject matter up to the tabulation first and then give you full instructions. The letter is to go to — capital A stop — Gipton *— I spell — capital* G — i — p *for Papa —* t *for Tango —* o — n *for November —* and Company Limited — Ten Ford Road — Barford — Yorkshire — For the attention of J — *stop —* Smith Esq — *Letter begins —* Dear Sirs — Further to our telephone conversation of the ninth of June — *comma —* and your request for details of the goods you propose to stock for resale — *comma —* I am now sending you a list of items — *full stop — new paragraph*

As you will see — *comma —* both wholesale and retail prices are clearly marked in the last two columns — *full stop — typist please — from this point I would like the tabulation to start. I require six columns — size of each column as follows: first column three and a half cm wide, second column one cm wide, third column, two cm wide, fourth column two cm wide, fifth column two cm wide, sixth column two cm wide. Headings as follows — Number one —* Product *— number two —* Type Number *— number three —* Size *— number four —* Material *— number five —* Wholesale Price *— number six —* Retail Price *— The contents are as follows — first line — column one —* egg cups *— column two —* capitals EC *— oblique four — column three —* four centimetres high *— column four —* Plastic *— column five* one pound fifty pence *sterling* per ten *— column six —* twenty five pence each *— second line — first column —* Butter dish *— second column —* capitals — BL *— oblique — six nine — third column —* eight by six centimetres *— fourth column —* Plastic —

fifth column – three point 00 per ten – *sixth column* – seventy-five pence each
– *third line* – *first column* – Cheese board – *second column* – capitals CB –
oblique – one eight – *third column* – ten by five centimetres – *column four* –
Wood – *column five* – six point twenty per ten – *column six* – one pound
twenty each – *line four* – *column one* – Bread basket – *column two* – capitals BB
– *oblique* – zero seven – *column three* – twelve centimetres diameter – *column
four* – wicker – *column five* – seventy-five pence each – *column six* – one
pound fifty pence each – *line five* – *column one* – Egg spoons – *column two* –
capitals ES – *oblique* – one three – *column three* – six centimetres long –
column four – stainless steel – *column five* – eighty pence per ten – *column six*
– twenty pence each – *line six* – *column one* – Beakers – *column two* – capital B
– *oblique* three three – *column three* – seven centimetres high – *column four* –
Earthenware – *column five* –three point fifty per ten – *column six* – seventy-
five pence each –

Typist that completes the entries for the tabulation – *next paragraph* – Delivery of
goods will be three weeks from receipt of order – *End of letter* – *signed* Yours
faithfully – *thank you typist.*

A. Gipton & Company Limited
10 Ford Road
Barford
Yorkshire

For the attention of J. Smith Esq

Today's date

Dear Sirs,

Further to our telephone conversation of 9 June, and your request for details of the goods you propose to stock for resale, I am now sending you a list of items.

As you will see, both wholesale and retail prices are clearly marked in the last two columns.

Product	Type No	Size	Material	Wholesale price	Retail price
Egg cups	EC/4	4cm high	Plastic	£1.50 per 10	25p each
Butter dish	BL/69	8 × 6cm	Plastic	£3.00 per 10	75p each
Cheese board	CB/18	10 × 5cm	Wood	£6.20 per 10	£1.20 each
Bread basket	BB/07	12cm diam	Wicker	75p each	£1.50 each
Egg spoons	ES/13	6cm long	Stainless Steel	80p per 10	20p each
Beakers	B/33	7cm high	Earthenware	£3.50 per 10	75p each

Delivery of goods will be three weeks from receipt of order.

Yours faithfully,

A Gordon
Sales Department

18 Dictation on to preprinted forms

It is a requirement within some organizations to dictate matter on to preprinted forms. This method of dictation can easily be achieved provided the audio typist has a prototype form in front of her acting as a guide. If there are many different forms being used, it is beneficial to code them for identification purposes.

When dictating the text it is important to inform the typist to which question the entry is being supplied. Below is an example of preprinted form dictation.

Good morning typist, this is Mr J Brown of the Transfer Department, extension number 445. This is a preprinted form – code number X for X-ray – oblique – twenty-one. Would you please make two copies – the form is for redirection of mail. Question one – name of the company – please type all entries in capitals – John Blinker & Company Limited *– Question two – on the left-hand-side –* Twenty-four Adams Street *–* Hessleton *– typist please – postal code – in capitals –* HES *figures* one *–* two *–* three *– on the right-hand side for new address –* Blinker House *–* The Maize *– I spell –* M *for Mike –* a *–* i *–* z for Zulu *–* e *–* Phrampton *– I spell – capital P for Papa –* h *–* r *for Romeo –* a *–* m *for Mike –* p *–* t *–* o *–* n *for November –* Middletown *– typist – postal code – capitals* MID *– in figures* 456 *– Question three – please tick box C. Question four, will you fill in where it states – Name and address on Licence – typist give the company name and address – the old address and the new address. Question five, will you fill in where it states – Redirection to start from – seven a.m. – first of January 1990. Question six, please tick. Question seven please delete b & c. End of dictation – thank you.*

The Post Office

Royal Mail Redirection Service

The Postmaster

Please redirect mail as indicated

Please read Note 2

1 Names of persons requiring redirection

Name or names (State title Mr/Mrs etc and initials)

Please use capital letters

Title	Initials	Surname	Signature
		JOHN BLINKER &	
		COMPANY LIMITED	

For firms, the business name should be shown followed by the signature of the Secretary or other authorised person. For households, all persons **must** give a signature.

(Warning: Criminal diversion of postal packets from an addressee is an offence under Section 56 of the PO Act 1953. The penalty is a fine not exceeding £500 or imprisonment for a term not exceeding six months or both.)

2 Address to which mail should be redirected

Please use capital letters

Old address (in full):

24 ADAMS STREET

HESSLETON

Postcode HES 123

New address (in full):

BLINKER HOUSE

THE MAIZE

PHRAMPTON   MIDDLETOWN

Postcode   MID 456

Please read Note 5 for detailed explanation of options available

3 Period of redirection required

Please tick the appropriate box

Applications for an initial redirection period

| A | | B | | C ✓ |

Applications for extended redirection

| D | | E | | F |

Fee payable £

4 Amendment to the address on your television licence

Please complete this section in CAPITAL LETTERS if your change of address is permanent and you want details of your television licence transferred to your new address.

Name shown on licence: JOHN BLINKER & COMPANY LIMITED

Old address shown on licence:

24 ADAMS STREET

HESSLETON

Postcode   HES 123

New address:

BLINKER HOUSE

THE MAIZE

PHRAMPTON   MIDDLETOWN

Postcode   MID 456

Television licences are not transferable from one person to another, but if you are changing your name on marriage please enter your new name here.

Change of name:

3

please turn over

5 Starting date

Redirection is to start from   7 a.m. 1 January   19 90

If the change of address is temporary,
please also give the finishing date   19

6 Parcels

See Note 4

Please tick this box if you require parcels to be redirected. If this box is left blank parcels will be treated as undeliverable and returned to sender(s)

| ✓ |

7 Fees

See Note 6

I wish to pay the fee due by (please delete as appropriate):

a   Cheque made payable to 'The Post Office'.

~~b   Girobank transfer to the Head Postmaster's Girobank account.~~

~~c   Postage stamps which are affixed in the space below and cancelled with my signature.~~

8 I note that The Post Office reserves the right to refuse to redirect mail and/or to discontinue this redirection order at any time.

Signature _____   19

For completion at the delivery office serving old address

1 Request recorded on P553B	2 Acknowledgement letter sent	3 Sent to Postcode Duty	4 (if applicable) Recorded in Accounts Branch for payment to Subpostmaster
Initials	Initials	Initials	Initials
Date	Date	Date	Date

Retention period: 1 year after expiry date

Do not detach

For attention at Delivery Office serving old address

Send complete form to Postcode Duty.

For attention at Postcode Duty

Check Postcode details, detach this section and forward it to
National TV Licence Records Office, BRISTOL BS98 1TL.

For attention at NTVLRO

Transfer licence details from old to new address and change name if necessary.

4   OP/01368 2/88

19 Instructions for word processing applications

Edited draft

Hello Mary, George Brown here – I have altered the draft you typed for me. Just a few instructions to make my editing quite clear. You will find that a number of paragraphs have been shifted from their original position. I have marked these by numbering them. I have also changed various items within each paragraph, also numbered. The figures appearing in the text were slightly underestimated, so to make it quite clear, I have marked it with coloured pen. I think we need another draft before final printing to make absolutely sure that all is quite clear. Thank you Mary.

These instructions will be dictated to Mary and passed to her with the altered draft which she will now copy type by returning the original text on to her screen and making the required alterations. With this kind of draft alteration, it will always be useful to produce dictated instructions which help to clarify the updates.

Programmed correspondence

Using the Dictation Manual in which all standard paragraphs, sentences, words etc. have been entered, instructions can be made in the following manner:

Hello Mary, George Brown here. As you know, we are launching the new Sproggets, incorporating the variable controls and I want to inform some of our existing customers about availability. I want to concentrate on the Midland Region initially, so can you use the lists for Birmingham, Coventry, Stratford and Stoke, The paragraphs I need are as follows:

Paragraph 1 – please insert the product name – Acorn – followed by codes –

Universal, Original and Speedwell – *Paragraph 7* – *When you come to the sentence 'discounts as follows' please insert the figures which I have included with this recording on the blue copy sheet* – *Paragraph 9* – *please insert my name in place of the one on the original recording.*
This letter will be included with the new brochures. When you have printed out the new version, I'll check it and you can then send it to the Public Relations Department for insertion and mailing. Thank you Mary.

In this way using prerecorded paragraphs the operation of composing a personalized sales letter will help speed up the production of correspondence for the launch.

PART IV

INSTALLATION OF A DICTATING SYSTEM

20 Note form dictation

The micro-based portable dictation machine, a now highly sophisticated addition to the dictation systems range and often described as a Pocket Note Taker, is a constantly attentive ear and reminder, any time, anywhere. And if everyone makes proper use of it, the machine can form part of a total communication system.

The use of note form dictation has increased greatly over the years and its applications have changed from pure correspondence to all manner of reminders and aids to the production of multi-tasks.

Some organizations, whose staff are engaged in duties such as insurance claim assessments or stocktaking, find the use of note-taking dictation equipment very worthwhile. The need to handle paper and pen or pencil is kept to a minimum and the subject matter is dictated into a small portable machine instead.

Instructions to the audio secretary can be kept to a minimum since the contents of the dictation are usually produced in draft form. In this way corrections can be made on the draft by the author and then either redictated with all relevant instructions or presented for copy typing.

The most important instruction when using this form of dictation is the identification at the start of the sequence since the medium is often posted back to the company after working on location and transcribed in the dictater's absence.

A very effective way of maximizing the use of the Note Taker is within the manager–secretary partnership or multi-team situation where a secretary may be working for several managers. Instead of communicating verbally, little yellow reminder notes are stuck to all manner of office surfaces. The use of the Note Taker allows both managers and secretaries an alternative to face-to-face exchanges, with the facility to enlarge on any message or information. All that passes between them is the micro-cassette. And in a multi-manager situation the method can be even more efficient since the simultaneous presence of all managers in the office is very rare indeed. Even manager-to-manager communication can benefit by using the Note Taker and, if necessary, the contents can still be transcribed in draft form.

A very useful application is for managers to have such a machine on their bedside tables when they retire at night, in order to capture those fleeting ideas occurring in the middle of the night, which may have vanished by morning. Or perhaps important inclusions need to be remembered which, with a few dictated words, can act as invaluable reminders.

Listed below are some of the functions for which note-taking dictation equipment can be very effective:

- stocktaking
- insurance claim assessment
- salesman's report away from base
- reports while at meetings
- note-taking while on training courses
- survey work
- hospital visits by medical staff
- home visits by nursing staff
- architectural site work
- factory inspection
- police work
- office team communication

21 The input stage to word processing

These days, most organizations use word processing machines in one form or another. These systems provide a very valuable contribution to paper production within all manner of departments and applications are constantly being updated and newly designed. Some of the more sophisticated word processing systems provide arithmetical capabilities and can often double up as a general purpose office machine.

Word processing allows dictated matter to be entered in draft form and provides the facility to correct, alter, change sequences and generally edit the draft so that the final result will be a perfect document. And since the dictated matter, once keyed in, is recorded, it can be recalled and reprinted at any time in the future.

Once a draft has been produced, recorded and submitted to the author, it can be corrected and changed into an acceptable document. Obviously, a draft with appropriate corrections will then become a copy typing job – it would be very expensive and time consuming to redictate all the alterations.

If any information related to the corrected work needs to be brought to the audio secretary's attention, the author should dictate the instructions and hand the recording to her together with the relevant sheets of the corrected draft. However, one word of warning. The fact that the facility to correct any text exists without having to retype the whole document, even if it only applies to a small word or punctuation sign, does not mean that this gives you licence to become too fastidious and drive the audio secretary mad. Between you, do come to an agreement about the number of times a document can be returned for yet another small alteration. It is all very well to strive for perfection, but eventually the document will have to move on.

Some organizations use a great number of preprinted forms, and the word processor can be used for formatting. Once a particular format has been designed and programmed, the appropriate form may be called up on-screen when required, and the dictated details may be infilled by the audio secretary. The author will usually have a specimen format which can be used as an *aide-memoire* to help dictate the appropriate text into the right spaces on the form. If the infills are too complex, then previous rules would apply. Provide the audio secretary with your format copy already filled in and add your dictated instructions (for dictation procedures, see Chapter 18).

A particularly popular application is 'Programmed Correspondence', so called because it enables text to be broken down into standard paragraphs, sentences, product titles, salutations etc. These are recorded on a 'building block' principle, providing a less stereotyped, but highly productive, correspondence system. In every office there will be some letters which are so different from others that they will, under any system, have to be treated as 'one-offs'. But there will also be many which say virtually the same thing in slightly different ways, depending on the originator. It is these which can often be programmed, following a detailed analysis of a representative selection of the organization's outgoing mail.

The next step is to agree the wording of the standard paragraphs to be used. In the interest of maximizing productivity later on, it is advisable to create separate blocks even for the most minor variations thus avoiding the necessity for further manual infills. Of course, these cannot be avoided altogether if letters are to be completely personalized but they should be kept to a minimum. Once the library of standard terms has been agreed and checked, it can be entered into the word processor and printed out after coding. It is these codes which the author will use when dictating, simply recording the required codes and any variables which may be required. The printed form will simply be used as an *aide-memoire*. It would be very advisable to produce a *Correspondence Manual* – the author's book of reference – from which he will select the particular building blocks he needs to compose a letter on any subject covered by the Programmed Correspondence System. His instructions to the audio secretary may be given on this kind of form or he may dictate his selections and any necessary variables on tape.

Using this particular approach, the actual letter production becomes a simple two-step operation. First, the selections and variables are typed. The list may be sent back to the author for checking if desired. Then, if continuous stationery is used, the letters themselves can be produced very quickly and accurately in an entirely unattended operation. Using this approach, typing productivity can be increased up to tenfold. What is more, the originators will become more productive and, just as important, become more consistent in what they say and thus better able to reflect company policy or avoid ambiguity. Of course everyone concerned has to know exactly how the system works and what they are expected to do so that coordination between author and audio secretary is maximized.

The possibilities for the use of word processing techniques are indeed endless and there is no better way of improving a company's image than by insisting upon standards of presentation and accuracy, difficult to achieve without the aid of modern word processing equipment, coupled with the use of an efficient dictation system. To achieve the best results, the guidelines listed below should be followed.

1 Unless a word processor is used for all typing matter, which includes two- or three-line memos, instructions to the audio secretary need not be quite as detailed as when a conventional typewriter is used.
2 When correcting drafts, do come to an amicable understanding about the number of times corrections can be made.
3 Make sure that, when giving back corrected matter which contains dictated instructions, the details clearly indicate which corrected draft the dictation refers to.
4 When dictating on to preprinted forms, familiarize yourself with the format on the word processing screen and watch when the entries are carried out. This helps future dictation know-how.
5 Where Programmed Correspondence procedures are used, communicate with the audio secretary fully, obtaining information on how codes should be indicated. This must be a combined exercise so that all concerned are fully aware of the methods used to instruct requirements.
6 If you have any particular needs for unusual applications, do involve the audio secretary. She is often capable of designing suitable software programmes for your use.

Checklist of some word processing applications

- standard letter production;
- legal documents with different variations;
- technical and other reports;
- Programmed Correspondence;
- storage and retrieval of preprinted business forms;
- reformatting of text;
- building up of composite documents, i.e. specifications, quotations, tenders etc.,
- arithmetical capability – processing words and numbers simultaneously;
- word processing/reprographics;
- data transmission online from word processors to computers.

22 The importance of dictation equipment

In this age of information technology and office automation, word processing has become increasingly a part of an office environment. But the smooth and rapid process of words from thought to composition, to dictation then transcription, printing and distribution is too often slowed at the input or dictation stage. Indeed, slow and inefficient input will negate the benefits of the rapid output, now achievable with screen-based equipment and high-speed printers.

The alternatives to using dictation equipment are a little like walking backwards to the airport before flying Concorde across the Atlantic.

1 Dictation equipment will help you convert thoughts into correspondence *rapidly*.
2 Dictation equipment will assist you to 'talk' work off of your desk *rapidly*.
3 Dictation equipment provides an *escape* from high cost and inefficient processing of words and correspondence.
4 Dictation equipment gives *economy, speed, convenience, accuracy, productivity,* and *flexibility*.

- *Economy*. Cost saving, whilst difficult to measure precisely, can be quantified when related to time saved both by dictaters and secretaries and by the unnecessary duplication of effort involving two people simultaneously engaged in shorthand dictation. A most conservative estimate would indicate anticipated savings of at least 30 per cent.
- *Speed*. Time taken writing shorthand, an exercise frequently lengthened by irritating interruptions and telephone calls, is eliminated.
- *Convenience*. Using a dictation machine, the dictater has the facility of dictating letters 24 hours a day. There is no question of waiting whilst the secretary finishes typing previous dictation, or waiting until she comes back from lunch. Nor are there delays caused by illness. He can

record ideas whenever/wherever they occur to him. Similarly, a secretary is not interrupted in the middle of a task by being summoned to take shorthand.

- *Accuracy*. What was said at the time of dictation is clearly recorded and can be referred to at any time, unlike shorthand notes which tend to go stale after a time and, in the case of illness, can often not be read by a secretary's colleague.
- *Productivity*. One person instead of two is involved in the dictation exercise and the time saved by both provides an opportunity for increased output or completion of additional tasks.
- *Flexibility*. Dictation machines provide the ultimate in flexibility; their use enables dictated material to be shared among the audio typists available. This is unlike shorthand which tends to be confined to one secretary's notes. Again, what secretary is available at such varied times and is in as many locations as a machine?

Types of equipment

Portables

Small, compact and lightweight, these are now generally pocket-sized and are ideal for out of office use. Easily operated they provide excellent means of recording notes, interviews, reports and dictating correspondence whilst the user is on the move. They ensure that office efficiency is maintained even outside the office.

Desk Tops

Either for recording use by the dictater or transcription use by the secretary, desk top models provide the ultimate in features and benefits. Not only will they be available at any time during the working day, they will cope efficiently with high-volume work all day.

Centralized systems

Increasingly used within word processing centres, centralized systems can bring enormous increases in efficiency. In the right circumstances, they will provide total concentration on the rapid production of correspondence, the best possible distribution of work amongst typists and the fastest possible turnround of dictated material. A centralized system enables you to convert thoughts into correspondence via a telephone, whether that instrument is in your office, in a hotel room or in a call box.

Checklist for action

1 Examine how your company copes with correspondence at present.
2 Objectively determine the shortcomings or inefficiencies of that system.
3 Determine the exact objectives/criteria to be met by any new system introduced.
4 Determine whether needs will be properly met by introducing portable, desk top or centralized equipment, or maybe a mix of these.
5 Discuss your needs with outside consultants if there are no qualified people capable of handling such an exercise within the organization.
6 Draw the secretaries into the discussion; they are the users of such equipment at the production end, and can contribute valuable ideas.

23 The text processing manager

There are many essential attributes inherent in an effective text processing manager or supervisor who, after all, makes a very real contribution to good management and smooth working. These attributes can be brought out by means of attendance at training courses of which there are a number available. No matter whether the staff is large or small, a well chosen and trained manager in charge of text processing, both from input through to output, can be worth a premium salary. Failure to direct procedures both in a word processing centre or where individual correspondence secretaries are employed can quickly produce chaos or, at best, a lack of direction which can produce misunderstandings among the staff and lack of know-how leading to frustration amongst the authors.

Not only must the manager herself be a competent typist with experience of secretarial working at all levels, but she must also possess ability as an organizer of staff, be tactful in her handling of them and fair in her outlook in relation to the distribution of the workload. She is the link between management and those concerned with the output of correspondence, and her knowledge, alertness and ability to decide priorities will often be taxed if the whole organization is to run smoothly and efficiently.

Many problems can be avoided if executives make a point of taking this manager into their confidence and drawing her into their discussions affecting any change in policy and method. In this way she can familiarize herself with the firm's terminology, its mode of operation, the standard forms to be used and the order of priorities required by management.

An experienced and able text processing manager has much to offer any organization and her advice can prove invaluable, especially in times of stress. She will undoubtedly have a good working knowledge of the system adopted in the organization and the characteristics of the equipment. Often her advice on further training given to staff will pay dividends by cutting costs. She will also be able to monitor, advise and even retrain the company's authors in dictation procedures. Additionally, she can be the means (if she is allowed to express herself freely) of avoiding many of the errors and deficiencies of dictaters which can be so frustrating in a busy office.

She might even tender the advice outlined below, which was drawn up in desperation by a very experienced supervisor, in the hope that dictaters would accept a not-too-subtle hint!

Rules for dictaters

1   Please keep a cigarette or pipe in your mouth when dictating. It aids pronunciation.

2   Please admire your walls and ceiling and floor while dictating. This enables your voice to come over loud and clear and soft and in fits and starts.

3   If another person is sharing your office, please make sure he is carrying on a loud conversation with someone or banging doors or drawers while you are dictating. It makes the audio secretary's job so much easier to distinguish your voice.

4   When dictating the name of a company such as 'Smith and Read', do make sure you spell 'Smith' and not 'Read' (Reid, Reede, Reed, Reide).

5   Please don't forget your 'ums' and 'just a minutes' after every second or third word. This gives the audio secretary a break.

6   Please don't forget to change your mind, and never never give instructions beforehand. This is unforgivable.

7   Please don't forget to say 'now where were we?' after dictating two or three paragraphs of a letter and then go back and redictate.

8   Please, when dictating from a written document, speak at least 180 words per minute. This enables the secretary to keep up with you and she will also be able to understand every word.

9   Whatever happens, never never say 'end of dictation' or 'please' or 'thank you'. A 'good morning' would, of course, be out of the question. These small courtesies are a dreadful waste of breath.

10   Please do not waste your energy by bringing us the files, even if you are coming to see us – more especially if you need the letter urgently. You, and perhaps half a dozen more, all want 'urgents' typed straight away, and of course at 4.30 or 5.00pm we have more time than you.

11   If your work is 'confidential' please make sure we get the message. After all, you must ensure great secrecy, so cut off your words before they are finished and make sure you lower your voice.

12   Please don't forget to tell us when you require a capital letter – especially after you are sure we have already typed the word.

13   Always quote a reference *after* the name and address. It doesn't

appear like that on the letter heading, but we like working back-wards.

14 Please bring a four- or five-page draft in at 5.15 to go out the same evening. We have not yet learnt to type with our feet, but no doubt this can be achieved.

15 Please do not announce who you are when you commence dictating. It is a great help to a new employee just to hear a reference and extension number and, sometimes, neither.

16 Never start work first thing in the morning. We prefer a great rush in the late afternoon.

17 Hours of dictation: during the lunch break and any time between 4.30 and 5.30pm.

18 Whenever possible, dictaters should endeavour to keep the secretary late. We have no homes to go to and are only too thankful to have somewhere to spend the evening.

19 Should work be required urgently (a most unusual occurrence), it aids the audio secretary considerably if the dictater rushes in at intervals of 30 seconds to see if it is done.

20 When making a tricky alteration which requires concentration and precision, always stand over the secretary and breathe down her neck whilst she does it.

Rules for audio secretaries

1 Never read your letters through after typing them as this only wastes your time. Let the boss waste his time correcting them, or, better still, let them go out incorrect.

2 Always try to put your letters in the wrong envelopes. It is a pleasant surprise for someone whose name is Bill to be addressed as Dear John and to be told some other firm's secrets.

Index

Applications for
  Word Processing, 93
  Note Taking, 90
Action on types of
  equipment, 96
Assistance from Text Processing
    Manager, 97
  General Hints, 98–99

Business Letters, 59
  examples, 60–65
Capital letters, 42
  initial and full, 42
Choice of system, 94
  suitability of equipment, 95
Confidential work, 4
Corrections, 31–32

Delivery, 25–27
Dictation Plan, 16–17
Dictation procedure, 14–15
Dictation routine, 12–13

External letters, 15
Equipment examples, 8–11

Figures, dictation of, 53–54
Final paragraph, 36
Fluency, aids to, 26
Form of address, 36

Headings, 38–39

Identification of dictater, 3–5
Indenting, 38–39
Instructions to typists, 23–24
  draft reports, 24
  letters, 23
  memos, 24
  tabulations, 24

Internal memos, 66
  examples, 67–70
Interruptions, 31–32

Length of dictation, 4
Logical preparation, 4–5

Money, amounts of, 53–54

Note form dictation, 89–90
Notes from dictaters, 12–22
Notes or headings, 10

Opening paragraphs, 36
Organization of material, 9–11

Pauses, 28–30
Phonetic alphabet, 41
Pitch of voice, 6–7
Posture, 25–27
Preparation for dictation sequence,
    8–11
Pre-printed forms, dictation onto,
    81–83

Punctuation, 43–45
    brackets, 47–51
    colon, 47
    comma, 45
    exclamation mark, 50–51
    full stop, 45
    hyphen, 48
    inverted commas, 51–52
    parentheses, 47
    question mark, 49
    quotation mark, 49
    semi-colon, 46

Reports, 15
    draft, 24
    finished, with special layout
        instructions, 71–77

Sequence of dictation, 13
    examples, 13
Similar sounding words, 55–56
Special layouts, 4–5
Speech, pitch of voice, 4–5
    use of natural voice, 6–7

Spelling, 40
Similar sounding words, 55–56
Supporting papers, 20–21

Text Processing Manager
    role, 98–99
    checklist of don'ts, 98–99
Tabulation, 37–39
Text organization, 35–39
    headings, 35–38
    body of letter, 36
    form of address, 36
    indents, 38
    opening paragraph, 36
    preparation, 36
Timing, 31–32
    interruptions, 28–29
    natural pauses, 30

Urgency of correspondence, 4
Underlining, 52

Volume control, 25